I'm Anxious and Can't Stop Overthinking.
Dialogues to Understand Anxiety, Beat Negative Spirals, Improve Self-Talk, and Change Your Beliefs

by Nick Trenton

www.NickTrenton.com

Table of Contents

Introduction 5
Session 1 13
Session 2 29
Session 3 49
Session 4 63
Session 5 79
Session 6 95
Session 7 107
Session 8 125
Session 9 141
Session 10 157
The Follow-Up Session 173
Becoming Your Own Therapist 183

Introduction

A qualified psychologist will always tell any new client the same thing, without fail: "What we talk about in our sessions stays in this room. Whatever you say will remain confidential."

In this book, however, we're going to get the chance to pull back the veil and peek into this private sanctuary so we can see exactly what therapy is, word for word, session by session. This is more than morbid curiosity, however; it's a chance to experience what therapy really is, from the inside out.

In the pages that follow, you'll be introduced to Leah, who has decided to seek help for a range of diffuse but distressing life problems, and Dr. Amanda, the therapist who will be accompanying her on her therapeutic journey, helping her navigate a path through those problems one step at a time.

Leah, of course, is not a real person. Neither is Dr. Amanda. Yet, their fictionalized dynamic interaction is, in a way, very real—it's inspired by countless real-life sessions with real people who have real concerns in day-to-day life. People like you and me.

Therapy is a unique place. Inside these quiet walls, something uncommon is happening. Therapy may look superficially like just "talk." But dig a little deeper and you'll see that it is a very specific kind of talk. Many of us are increasingly familiar with psychological terminology and the theory behind it. At the same time, we may seldom get the chance to see what those ideas look like when played out *in real life*. Therapy, simply, is a flowing dialogue.

It's not something you simply read about—it's something you do. Something you experience.

Since the earliest historical conception of talk therapy, people have understood that it's conversation—especially therapeutic conversation—that has the real power to bring insight into the way that people are thinking, feeling, and acting. What's more, this kind of conversation can act as a catalyst for doing something very exciting: change.

A good therapist is skilled at asking just the right questions at just the right time. They can listen for trigger words, become curious about inconsistencies, carefully challenge your assumptions, or gently guide your awareness to something you hadn't quite noticed before. In a very concrete way, a therapist helps you slow down so that you can think and feel "out loud." Working alongside you, they become your second brain, a pair of mental training wheels that help you keep your balance as you learn new skills, heal from old wounds, and steer your life back in the direction you want it to go.

Self-help books, blog posts, and journal articles are all great ways of exposing yourself to interesting new information. But they can never replace this interactive, dynamic, therapeutic relationship. They will never reflect anything back to you. They cannot recreate the powerful, generative back-and-forth of a genuine discussion.

A self-help book—even a really good one—can never ask you a question or show real human interest in your answer. Understanding the content in a journal article doesn't make you any more skilled at mastering the problems it talks about. And a fact sheet you find online cannot *witness* you—it cannot reflect on the individual that you are right here, right now.

This is where this book comes in. Sadly, many of us will not be able to access the kind of life-enriching conversation that's possible in good therapy. That may be because we cannot afford it, we don't have access to it, or we've simply already tried it in the past but found ourselves with a practitioner who was under-skilled or not right for us. Raising your psychological awareness is always valuable, and reading up about things like depression and anxiety can be useful. At the end of the day, however, transformation, healing, and maturation are all things that happen outside the therapy room, off the page, and *out there*, in the real world—as messy and unpredictable as that world can be.

My hope is that in the chapters that follow, you'll not only enjoy the story of a person bravely working through the obstacles and challenges they face, but you'll also start to recognize some of yourself in the conversations that unfold. In glimpsing behind the scenes, you may find yourself developing compassion for Leah—and perhaps developing a lot more of it for yourself in the process.

It's true that no two people are the same; the person you see depicted in these pages may be very different from you in important ways. There are, however, more than a few fundamental similarities in the ways that we all become "stuck," wrestle with our demons, and gradually find ways to open a window in our awareness and begin to see things in a new way. As you watch Leah improve in fits and starts, make breakthroughs, relapse and then break through again, wrestle with self-doubt, and contend with shame, vulnerability, and uncertainty, you may discover that your own attitude to those phenomena in yourself changes.

Eminent psychologist Albert Bandura had a theory of "social learning" that posited that human beings are unique in their ability to watch others and learn from them vicariously. Through the stories and experiences we see in others, and by observing other people and modeling our behavior on theirs, we can expand our own skills. By reading this book, you are in effect practicing and rehearsing exactly the kind of dialogue that is at the heart of the transformative therapeutic experience.

As you read, pause now and again to see what you'd say next. Notice your own reactions to what Leah shares and how she behaves. Give yourself the opportunity to see what you think about the way the therapist deals with these things, and why. Now and then do you recognize the voice of Leah in yourself? In the same way, do you have your own internal version of Dr. Amanda the therapist, who is wise and kind and believes in the best in people?

At the end of each chapter/session, you'll be prompted to reflect on things in this way—think of it as a kind of meta-therapy for you to engage in. A few caveats before we dive in, however:

- There are many, many different kinds of therapy. Some of the techniques Dr. Amanda uses will be familiar to you, and some won't. Even if you don't like or understand an approach she takes, see if you can move beyond deciding whether it's good or bad, and simply become curious about why this way of doing things doesn't appeal to you personally right now. All these things are "grist for the mill"—meaning that any reaction you have may yield valuable insight if engaged with in a spirit of respectful, compassionate curiosity.
- That said, even though Amanda is a hypothetical therapist, I wanted to make her seem as real as possible—and that meant making her a unique, flawed human being with a few blind spots of her own! Bluntly, Dr. Amanda doesn't always get it right. Pay attention to where you think she takes the wrong path or says the wrong thing. Notice, especially, whether perfection is even necessary for growth and connection. Notice how Leah responds, how Dr. Amanda handles her own missteps . . . and how *you* might.

- Be mindful of your expectations. Real, in-person therapy is not a picnic. It's not meant to be. Some people, especially those who have never stuck with a therapist for longer than a few sessions, may assume that therapy is simply there to make you feel good. They may unconsciously believe that the therapist's job is to build them up, flatter them, soothe them, supply them with excuses and permissions, or validate their self-diagnoses. The truth, however, is that therapy is often difficult. It's sometimes scary, confusing, or just plain boring. It's not entertainment, it's not a product to be consumed, and it's not merely a friendly chat with someone who will, out of kindness, allow you to hold on to your illusions.
- What is presented in these dialogues is compressed for ease of reading—real transcripts of real therapy would be too long-winded to be readable. Suspend your disbelief, if you can, and imagine that the conversation presented here is more *illustrative* than it is strictly accurate.
- Finally, therapy also takes time—because growth and healing take time. So, as you read, be patient with Leah. She's doing important work; it's work that takes time and isn't always simple or glamorous. Be patient, too, with Amanda—she is not a wise guru on a mountaintop, but a human being. She has training and good intentions and is

doing her best. But again, she is a human being, and she is figuring it all out *with* Leah, not *for* her.

Session 1

It was a chilly October morning, and Leah didn't know if her hands were shaking because of the cold or because she was about to meet Dr. Amanda Lindhurst, the psychotherapist whom she had spoken to on the phone yesterday but hadn't yet met in person. *Was this a stupid idea? I can't believe how expensive this is. Maybe this was a mistake—after all, I bet she sees people who are really messed up all the time, not like me ...*

The door to the reception room opened, and Dr. Amanda appeared.

"Hello—it's Leah, isn't it? Please, won't you come in?"

Dr. Amanda didn't look quite like Leah had imagined. She was dressed quite plainly, and as they walked into her "office," she was surprised to see that her surroundings were just as ordinary. The only thing to suggest that this wasn't just a normal living room was the very obvious arrangement of the chairs—they were pushed to gently face one another at a forty-five-degree angle, and at once Leah was struck by the idea that the chairs were already engaged in a private session of their own.

The pair sat, and Leah perched on the edge of her seat, trying—and failing—to find somewhere to rest her gaze. She couldn't think of what to do or say, so she defaulted to her usual habit: apologizing.

"I'm sorry," she gushed. "I haven't done this before. I don't really know how we start or anything."

"That's perfectly okay. You're here now, and it's good to meet you."

She didn't say anything further, and Leah's heart was now very definitely pounding. Her face felt hot. In a flash, she decided that she hated therapy and was never coming back. This was just too awkward. Plus, it was really, really expensive.

"I'm not even sure if this is the right place for me, actually," Leah said. "I just . . . I just don't know what to do anymore, and I need some help. Everyone says you should get therapy, but I'm not super depressed or anything like that. It's just more like ... well ..."

Dr. Amanda didn't jump in to speak. Her face was quiet and calm. Leah could tell she was listening. Strangely, this freaked her out.

"Okay, well. The reason I'm here is because, I guess, I'm quite *shy*. I'm an introvert, you see. Like I said on the phone yesterday, I'm in my second year of my degree, but college has just been hell. I'm finding it really difficult to make friends. Dating is just ... a disaster. I don't know, maybe I have low self-esteem. I don't know. I mean, my childhood was fine, and like, I don't want to take any medications or anything like that ..."

Here, Dr. Amanda spoke. "It sounds to me like there are lots of things going on in your world right now."

Leah scoffed. "Lots of things? Only *everything*."

To her surprise, Leah found herself instantly emotional. She fought back a tear.

"I'm sorry . . ." she said, and quickly wiped it away.

"Leah, I can see that there are many things upsetting you right now. You've taken a big step today, coming to see me. That's probably a little scary, right, and maybe you're not sure about it?"

"Well, I'm sure you have, like, *real* patients come in here with real problems, and I'm just complaining about nothing, but . . ."

"You think your problems are not real enough for therapy? Well, why don't you tell me a little more about what the problem is before we decide it's not important?"

"Okay. Well . . . the problem is I'm shy. I'm too shy."

"You're too shy. Okay. Can you tell me about why you've come to therapy *now*? I'm wondering if something happened recently, something that made you feel you were too shy?"

"Well, I don't know. We had this presentation in our tutorial group. And I completely messed it up. It was so humiliating. Everyone could tell how nervous I was, and it was so embarrassing. I just felt their eyes on me, and I went blank. I couldn't speak. And they were all watching me and judging me. I felt like I wanted to curl up and die."

"What did it feel like in your body when all this was happening?"

"Well . . ." Leah struggled to explain the experience. How could she describe the choking, closing-in feeling in her throat? The burning shame on her cheeks? The sensation of her insides liquifying?

"I felt like . . . I felt like . . ."

"Maybe," said Dr. Amanda, "you could tell me what you feel right now as you remember that moment."

Leah blinked.

"As you sit on that chair, Leah, tell me what it feels like, thinking back to that moment."

Leah was suddenly aware of just how far forward she was sitting in her seat. It was as though she suddenly zoomed out and saw herself—hunched over, tense, neck craned, body curled in on itself. All at once she noticed how quickly she was speaking, how tight and small her voice was, how she was still avoiding eye contact. She straightened up a little and sat back into the seat.

"I feel . . . a little like I felt then. *Scared.* My heart's going really fast."

For a moment, neither of them said a word. Then, Dr. Amanda said, "Leah, I see a lot of people who experience anxiety of all kinds."

"Wait, *anxiety*? I don't have anxiety!"

"No?"

"No way. Like I said, I don't need medication or anything. I'm fine. Just a little shy."

"Are you worried that I'm going to suggest you take medication?"

"Well, I guess. I really don't want to."

"Don't worry, I certainly won't force you! Let's just take a breather for a moment here so I can explain what I do. I'm a cognitive behavioral therapist, which means I use a CBT approach. To put it very simply, what I do is look at you as a whole person, and that includes your thoughts, your feelings, and your behavior. You see, your thoughts influence your feelings, and your feelings influence your thoughts."

"And does your behavior influence your thoughts?"

"What do *you* think?"

Leah considered this.

"I think they all influence each other," she said at last.

"I think so too, Leah. And I think that even as we look at these three things and how they affect one another, we also need to look at what's going on around you—your environment. Because your environment is influencing you, but you can also in turn influence it. Does that sound like a reasonable way of thinking about things?"

Leah nodded.

"You've mentioned twice now the issue of medication. Now, that's certainly something that's appropriate for some people. There's nothing wrong with taking medication for an anxiety disorder or something else, but there's lots we can do together without it."

"I really don't want to. I'm not crazy," Leah said quickly.

Again, there was a pause in the conversation.

"In my work with people with anxiety, I sometimes slow everything right down so we can take a close look at the thoughts people are having. I'm sure you can guess why I'm so nosy about their thoughts, right?"

"Why?"

"Well, because their thoughts tell me a little bit about their feelings..."

"And their feelings tell you about their behaviors," said Leah, completing the thought.

"*Exactly*," said Dr. Amanda. She drew a small triangle in the air. "Thoughts, behaviors, emotions—they all influence one another."

Leah leaned back in the chair, trying to figure out what any of this had to do with her making a fool of herself in her tutorial group.

"A moment ago, you said something to me," continued Dr. Amanda. "You said *I don't want to take medication. I'm not crazy.*"

"Yeah..."

"Do you think you're crazy, Leah?"

"Well, no. I'm not. Obviously. But..."

"Yes?"

"Sometimes ... sometimes I guess I do things that maybe seem crazy to other people."

"Like struggle to give a presentation during your tutorial group?"

Leah said nothing.

"Sometimes," said Dr. Amanda, "when I'm feeling anxious, I have this thought: *People are going to think I'm crazy*. Have you ever had this thought?"

"I'm having it right now," said Leah with a dry laugh.

"You are?"

Leah balked. It was a joke she hadn't expected to be taken seriously.

"Well . . . kind of. I mean, maybe *you* think I'm crazy."

"Why would I think you're crazy?"

"I don't know . . . because I'm sitting here all stressed and strung out. I can't explain myself properly."

"So maybe you're thinking, *Dr. Amanda can see I'm stressed, and she thinks I'm crazy.*"

"Do you think that?"

"I'm curious to see if *you* think that."

Leah chewed her lip.

"The thing I'm thinking is not that exactly. It's more like . . . well, that everyone thinks I'm a loser. I'm an introvert. And people hate introverts."

"Do they?"

"Totally. They don't understand that it's harder for me."

"Socializing is harder? Why should it be harder for you?"

"Well, I don't know... I'm an introvert. I've never found it easy. And when people see you struggling, they hate it. They don't like introverts. It's a fact."

Dr. Amanda took a deep breath.

"Leah, can we try something quickly?"

"Sure."

"Remember what I said about the triangle? About how thoughts and feelings and behaviors are connected?"

"Yes."

"Well, I'm curious to understand how these beliefs fit into your life."

"What beliefs?"

"Well, the belief that you're a loser, that you're an introvert, and that people hate introverts."

"That's not a belief. That's just the truth."

"Okay. What I'm curious to know is how that makes you feel?"

Leah smirked.

"Yeah, I know . . . sometimes therapists really do ask that question!"

They both chuckled a little but quickly became serious again.

"What kind of emotions do you feel when you think the thought, *I'm a loser and an introvert and people hate me*?"

Leah was taken aback.

"I didn't say that people hate me."

"Didn't you?"

"Well, no, I guess I did. It's just . . ."

"It's quite a harsh thing to say about yourself, isn't it?"

"Yeah."

"How does it feel?"

"Well, obviously it feels awful!"

Outside, the light was fading.

"If you closed your eyes right now and thought, *Dr. Amanda hates me; everyone hates me*, what does that feel like in your body? Can you tell me?"

"It feels like . . . like I want to die. It feels so bad."

"I see you're slumped in your chair again."

Leah looked down. It was true.

"I feel so . . . small," she said. This surprised her. She hadn't thought of it that way before, but that was exactly what it felt like: smallness. When she thought people hated her, she felt tiny, insignificant, and invisible. Like a little, worthless, crushed thing.

"When you feel like that," continued Dr. Amanda, "when you feel small like that, what do you *do*? How do you act?"

This question somehow felt easier for Leah to answer, and she answered immediately.

"I do nothing. Absolutely nothing. I don't speak. I just hide in the background like a loser."

Quiet again.

"I wonder, then," said Dr. Amanda very slowly, "what exactly it is that's making you feel like a loser."

Leah immediately blurted out, "Other people . . . they hate me," but something strange happened as she did. She realized that she wasn't sure if she really believed it. Her voice trailed off.

The rest of the session passed quickly and uneventfully. Leah, feeling a little exposed and embarrassed, retreated somewhat, and the pair chatted comfortably about this and that until the hour is up. Leah agreed to see Dr. Amanda the following week and left, but as she walked into the reception area and out into the cool October night, she felt more confused than before. All on the journey home she found herself returning to memories of snippets of conversation—what exactly is it that made her feel like a loser? It was a strange question, and one that Dr. Amanda had not given her an answer to.

She turned the experience over in her mind again and again. Therapy had *not* been what she had expected. Dr. Amanda was far sweeter, far kinder than she had guessed, and she seemed to genuinely listen to what Leah had to say. At the same time, Leah was a little surprised at how Dr. Amanda hadn't seemed the least interested in her childhood and hadn't wanted to talk about her being an introvert.

She looked down at her lap at the printed-out exercise sheets that Dr. Amanda had assigned her for "homework." She'd scanned through them, and they seemed like kindergarten exercises. Did Dr. Amanda think she was some kind of moron? The hour had flown by, and they had talked so much, but Dr. Amanda hadn't diagnosed her with anything, or asked about any childhood trauma, or given her any kind of test . . .

Leah hadn't dared breathe a word to her about . . . the other stuff. The drinking. About her mother and the medication she had taken right up until her death and how it had scared Leah so badly she had vowed never to touch pills again, not even a Panadol for a headache. She definitely hadn't mentioned anything about Bradley, about how bad things had been last year, about any of it . . .

By the time Leah arrived at home, she had convinced herself that the only reason she'd felt a little better after the session was because she had successfully concealed from the doctor just what a mess she was. The therapist was nice and all, but she clearly had no idea what she was dealing with. This CBT stuff was bogus, anyway—it was just too simplistic for a person so badly messed up as Leah. At home she tossed the homework pages in the trash and told herself that she'd go to one more session, but no more. She kicked off her shoes, grabbed a beer from the fridge, and collapsed onto the sofa, where she scrolled through her phone for the next two hours.

Reflect

- What did you make of the first session between Leah and Dr. Amanda?
- What do you think Dr. Amanda was trying to get Leah to understand by explaining the "triangle" of thoughts, emotions, and behaviors?
- What is your response when Leah claims that "people hate introverts" is not a belief but plain fact? What would you say to her if she kept on insisting that she was upset *because* people hated her?
- Finally, what obstacles can you predict may pose a problem in the future for Leah and her time with Dr. Amanda?

Dr. Amanda is right—anxiety is pretty common. People tend to misunderstand what it means, however. Anxiety is more than "stress"—it's a state of prolonged unease, nervousness, and worry that occurs persistently in situations where there is no immediate threat. While fear is a natural physiological reaction designed to keep us safe, anxiety is a more generalized and continuous reaction of fear to things that are generally safe.

Anxiety can manifest itself in many different ways—in phobias and panic, in social anxiety (like Leah, as we'll see shortly), or in general worry and rumination that doesn't seem to settle on anything in particular. Anxiety is not "all in the head"—it's very much in the body! Faulty appraisals of threat in the environment trigger a cascade of chemical reactions in the body (the fight-or-flight response) that, when prolonged, can lead to symptoms like insomnia, muscle aches and pains, headaches, palpitations, shortness of breath, gut issues, irritability, and behaviors like constant checking, nail-biting, rumination, and reassurance seeking, to name just a few.

Leah has found herself with a therapist who practices CBT—which is the form of therapy most recommended for anxiety. CBT works by examining and gently reworking the negative core beliefs and thoughts that contribute to anxiety. Though medication is an option, there are plenty of ways to find relief without it, and things like exercise and meditation can be just as effective.

Session 2

"You know, I've been thinking about what you said last week, and I think you've got me all wrong."

Leah strode into the therapy room and was talking before she had even sat down. She did not seem to notice the slightly amused look on Dr. Amanda's face.

"Woah, slow down! *Hello*," Dr. Amanda said.

"Sorry, I'm being rude. Hello. I just . . . I've been thinking about what you said."

"Oh? And what did I say?"

Dr. Amanda pushed her glasses up her nose a little. Leah wondered at this—had she always worn glasses? She could not remember them from last time. Had she really overlooked them for the full hour?

Leah cleared her throat. She had been rehearsing a little speech in her head all week, but the moment she opened her mouth, the words came out a lot angrier than she had planned.

"You said to me that basically I'm making myself feel like a loser because thoughts influence the way you feel, right? So, the reason I feel like a loser is just because I *think* I'm a loser. But I've got to say, Dr. Amanda, I think you've really misunderstood me if you think that was what I was saying. And actually, I got to thinking about it, and I think you're wrong to blame me like that, blame *me* for being an introvert, for being upset . . . I can't help the way I am, you know . . ."

Dr. Amanda said nothing.

"So . . . ?" said Leah.

"So what?" said Dr. Amanda.

"So, I think you've got me wrong, that's all."

Again, Dr. Amanda said nothing.

Leah began to regret her outburst. And yet, she felt good that she had spoken up for herself. It was something she never, ever did.

"Okay, so I've got you wrong," said Dr. Amanda. "Then put me right." Here she leaned forward and picked up a pad of paper and pen, then poised herself ready to write. "Let's put it down on paper so we can both be clear about what we are and are not saying. What do you think?"

Leah gave her a sideways look. She had assumed Dr. Amanda would be annoyed with her, but she was surprisingly calm.

"Okay," she said.

"So, tell me," said Dr. Amanda, "what it is you think I think about you? Let's write it down."

"Well, okay. You think . . . you think that everything in my life is just fine and I'm making myself unhappy by thinking that I'm a loser. But it's not true."

Leah waited for the doctor to argue with her, but there was no sound but the scratching of the pen on paper.

"Anything else . . . ?"

"I'm not wrong to say that, you know. To say that people don't like me."

"Well, Leah, the last thing in the world I want is for you to feel like I am attacking or blaming you. That wasn't my intention, and it will never be my intention. But I can see that this has struck a nerve for you. Quickly remind me what degree you're doing—it's a science degree, isn't it?"

"It's chemistry, yes."

"So, would I be right to assume that you know a little something about hypotheses? About the scientific method?"

"Of course."

"Good. That's good. Let's try this again and see if we can get a little further with it. Will you try an experiment with me? Obviously not exactly like a scientific experiment, but one not far off."

"Sure, okay. I guess. But I think I know where you're going with this . . ."

"You do?"

"Yeah. I read up on CBT last night."

"So, what do you think I'm about to suggest?"

"I don't know. You're going to argue with me, I guess, and tell me that I actually don't have any evidence for what I think and believe . . ."

"What would you have said then, if I told you that you didn't have evidence for the things you thought?"

"Well . . ." Here Leah got flustered. "That's the thing, I *do* have evidence. Lots and lots of evidence. All my life people haven't liked me. I'm not stupid. I can tell."

"So, the people who were at that presentation you told me about, the one where you couldn't find your words and got really embarrassed. Can we go back to them? Did they not like you?"

"They hated me."

"I see. And you have evidence for this? I certainly wouldn't stop you from believing something you have evidence for."

"Yes, I do have evidence. They were all staring at me with these, like, horrible looks on their faces . . ."

"I see! And that's when they told you they didn't like you?"

"No, they didn't say anything. They didn't have to."

"So, what's the evidence?"

"I just told you! The way they looked at me . . . the way that . . ." Leah cut herself short. "Look, I'm not an idiot. I can tell."

"Leah, I want you to understand me here—I'm sure that in that moment, you *felt* really bad. I have no doubt about that. I just wonder how you could possibly know what the other students were thinking. You're a smart woman. But I'm pretty sure you can't read minds."

Leah said nothing. She folded her arms and stared out the window.

"But, for the sake of arguing, let's say you're right," continued Dr. Amanda. "Let's say they don't like you. Maybe they *were* thinking that."

Leah shot her a look. "What? That doesn't seem like something a good therapist should say!" She laughed.

"Why not?"

"I don't know. I can't come in here and say all these bad things and then ... you agree with me!"

"Well, I'm not saying it's true. But I'm curious about this thought. You mentioned it today, and you mentioned it last time, too. *People don't like me. People hate me.* I don't know you, and I can't say with any certainty what those students were thinking in the tutorial that day. But I think these thoughts tell us more about you than they tell us about them."

"How do you mean?"

"Well, there's an exercise I do with my clients sometimes where we try to drill down to their core beliefs. Would you like to try it with me?"

"Okay. But . . ."

"Hm?"

"Well, I'm sorry for being a bit touchy about all this."

"It's okay, Leah. I know this stuff can be kind of outside the comfort zone. We're here and we're figuring this stuff out together, right?"

"Right."

"So, let's look at my little paper here. I wrote down some things you told me. Can I read them back to you?"

"Okay."

"It says, I'm an introvert. People hate introverts. Now—bear with me—do you think it's really true that people hate introverts? Hate is a pretty strong word."

"But they do, though."

"Well, I'm an introvert. Do you hate *me*?"

"Of course not!"

"Okay. So maybe we can change this statement a little...?" Dr. Amanda's pen got scratching on the page again, and she held up a new sentence, written in big, neat block capitals. It said PEOPLE SOMETIMES HATE INTROVERTS.

"What do you think?" she asked Leah. "Do you think this new version is reasonable?"

Leah nodded.

"Actually, I'm still not happy about this word *hate*, though. Can we think of a slightly less harsh word?"

"Let's put *dislike*, then," Leah said. "But some people do hate introverts. Just maybe not all of them do."

Dr. Amanda nodded and the pen scratched softly on the paper.

They both looked down at the words. SOME PEOPLE SOMETIMES DISLIKE INTROVERTS.

Dr. Amanda took a deep breath.

"Leah, do you remember last session, you told me how it felt when you had the thought that people hated you? Do you remember?"

"Yeah. I said it made me feel small."

"Exactly. Small. You said it made you feel really bad. Let's see how this thought compares. Can you read it for me?"

"What . . . out loud?"

Leah cleared her throat and read the words on the paper. Then she read them again.

"How do you feel? Still small?"

Leah paused. She was surprised—she didn't feel much at all. It seemed like a reasonable, fairly boring sentence.

"But . . . I don't get it. Do we stop there?" Leah said. "Don't you want me to keep re-writing it until it says, I don't know, something positive?"

"Positive?"

"Like, I don't know. Give me an affirmation or something. *Introverts are amazing just as they are*—something like that."

"Do you believe that?"

"Not really."

"Me neither."

For the second time that session, Leah felt herself feeling very surprised. "Some people sometimes dislike introverts"? *That* was the big, empowering result of the exercise?

"But . . . so you're saying that some people some of the time *will* actually dislike me?"

"That seems extreme to you? Yet a moment ago you were telling me that they *all* did."

Leah laughed. "You got me there. I just . . ."

"Tell me. What does it feel like when you think this new thought, *some people sometimes dislike introverts*?"

"It doesn't make me feel small and bad, I agree. But it just . . . feels wrong somehow."

The pause seemed to last an eternity.

"Leah, can you complete this sentence for me? I think that people should . . ." And she paused.

"People should . . ." Leah thought for a moment. "Well, people should be kind to me. People should like me for who I am?"

"Okay," said Dr. Amanda. "Let's slow down and have a look at this idea. This thought. People should like me for who I am. I'm going to ask you now to treat this thought as though it were a hypothesis."

"Yes..." Leah said, and nodded her head. "That's what I read up about last night, when I researched all this online, you know? They said CBT is about challenging your thoughts."

"Exactly. I mean, I always thought *challenge* sounded a little rude, so I like to think of it as more like a discussion. More like just putting ideas in the interview seat and seeing whether they're really worth your belief."

Leah laughed.

"What's so funny?"

"Well, I thought that this was going to go completely differently. I thought I was going to say *everyone hates me* and then you would argue with me and try to convince me that I was wrong, because... because..."

"Because what?"

"Well, I don't know. Because I'm amazing and lovable exactly as I am? I thought you were going to try to tell me that my self-esteem was low, that I needed to love myself and all that."

"Hmm..." said Dr. Amanda. "I have the feeling you really would have hated that."

"Well... it just feels phony. Like, it doesn't make sense to me to just *say* how much you love yourself, and how you're just fine and perfect as you are and everything's okay . . . and yet you don't really believe it. I guess I've misunderstood what CBT is."

"You're clearly very smart, Leah. I like the fact that you're asking questions about all this. You don't take anyone's word for it, do you? What I'm trying to do is show you that you shouldn't automatically take *your own* word for it, either."

Leah rubbed her head and tried to think. "So . . . you say I should treat this idea as a hypothesis. This idea that everyone should like me."

"Yes. You got it. Right now, it looks to me like an opinion, but you talk as though it were a fact. So would you be willing to take a closer look and see whether it really is a fact?"

"I mean, there's a chance I am actually right, though . . . isn't there?"

Dr. Amanda smiled. "There's only one way to find out!"

Leah smiled and, for the first time, felt like she was getting into this therapy thing.

"Maybe . . ." said Leah, "we should write this down, too?"

"Good thinking," said Dr. Amanda, and began to scribble it down. PEOPLE SHOULD LIKE ME.

They both stared at the words on the page. Somehow, seeing them written down there like that made the whole idea seem so much . . . smaller. Leah noticed how much better it felt to write it down, and how, with both her and Dr. Amanda staring down at it like a team, it felt like just a word puzzle, just a little word game to figure out.

"The thing I'm thinking about," said Dr. Amanda, "is that there have to be some people in your world that *you* don't like."

"Sure." Leah laughed. "Loads."

"Okay. Good. Can you think of just one of them? You don't have to tell me who it is."

Leah pondered to herself and then nodded her head.

"Now, can you tell me exactly why you dislike this person?"

"Well . . . I don't know. She's kind of annoying. I always found her a little bit of an attention-seeker, you know? She's very loud."

"Okay. And you don't like her much."

"Nope."

"Well, what if I told you that you *should* like her?"

"Well . . . I'd say I just . . . don't."

"Yeah? So . . . who's wrong in this scenario? Is it you or is it this other girl?"

"Who is *wrong*? Uh . . . I don't know. Nobody's wrong. I just don't like her."

"So, she is who she is, and you don't like her."

"I guess so."

"And that's not a problem?"

"Well . . . it's not a problem, I guess not. I mean, she's always going to be who she is."

"What if she demanded that you like her?"

"I just . . . wouldn't!" Leah laughed.

"I think you can see where I'm going with this," said Dr. Amanda.

Leah was quiet for a while. "You're saying that I have a right to dislike other people, so . . . they have a right to dislike me?"

"Well, what do you think about that?"

"I mean . . . it still doesn't feel good to have people dislike you."

"No, I never said it felt good. I just said that people are allowed to dislike who they dislike. *You're* allowed to dislike who you dislike, after all."

"But..."

"Let's go a little further. You have this belief—and it is a belief—that people should like you. But let me ask you now, what's so bad about people not liking you?"

Leah scoffed. "What's so bad about it? Isn't it obvious? It feels horrible."

"Okay. But why, exactly? What makes it horrible? If people don't like you, then it would mean..."

"It would mean..." said Leah. "It would mean that they thought I was bad somehow."

"And? What's so terrible about that?"

Leah stammered. "It's bad because... then I'd be excluded. I'd be like an outcast."

"Being an outcast. Why is that a problem? What does it imply if people decide to exclude you?"

"I don't know!"

"Think about it. Why does the idea of them excluding you hurt? What does it imply?"

"Well, it implies that I'm . . . bad. That I'm less than they are."

A tear rolled down Leah's cheek. There was silence.

"If people don't like me, it means I'm bad," said Dr. Amanda quietly. Then she repeated the sentence more slowly.

The words hung between them, dark and heavy. Leah felt exhausted and upset.

"I know these things are difficult to talk about," said Dr. Amanda, "but some people like to call these deeper ideas *core beliefs*. They're the more fundamental ideas we have underneath all our everyday thoughts. We all have our beliefs and ideas about other people, the world, ourselves. The trouble is that sometimes these core beliefs are not very reasonable, and sometimes they work against us."

Leah said nothing for the longest time. Then the clock on the wall caught her eye—the session had already run over by two minutes. Almost reading her mind, Dr. Amanda nodded and stood. They both took their time walking to the door, Leah still processing the discussion.

"Before you go, though," Dr. Amanda said, "did you manage to complete the homework I gave you last week?" Then, seeing Leah's expression, she smiled and continued. "Would you like to complete it and bring it with you next week?"

Leah nodded. She had not planned to come back after this session. She had not planned on ever completing the "homework." But now, she had to admit that there might be something here, something worth returning to.

"Yes. I'll bring it. Thank you so much, Dr. Amanda."

"Thank you."

Reflect

- What did you think of the session? Was there anything in particular that stood out to you?
- What do you think about Leah's expectation that she would be given an "affirmation" and encouraged to believe that she's perfect just the way she is?
- What do you think the difference is between *challenging* a thought and *questioning* it?

The technique that Dr. Amanda used in this session has many names but is sometimes referred to as the "downward arrow" technique. It's a method of using targeted questions to drill down to a person's core beliefs—those fundamental ideas and thoughts that inform and shape all other ideas and thoughts.

Leah had a core belief that went something like: **If people don't like me, then it means I'm a bad person.**

In fact, there is an even deeper, more fundamental level to this belief, which is simply: I'm a bad person. If someone were to believe this on a fundamental level, then they may consequently believe that external validation is necessary for them to be considered a worthwhile human being—and that's why not having this external validation is such a big problem! Someone who had a core belief that they were fundamentally a good person might be able to tolerate someone else's dislike for them because they knew that external opinion didn't define who they ultimately were.

Dr. Amanda could have merely said, "You're fine as you are!" but Leah would have instantly rejected this as "phony." We can see why—everything in the world is interpreted through the lens of our core beliefs. If Dr. Amanda had simply *told* Leah that she was a good person, Leah would have filtered this through her preexisting beliefs and concluded that Dr. Amanda was lying or just plain wrong. This is why CBT is not just about arguing with people on an intellectual level to try to convince them of the irrationality of their beliefs. Instead. Dr. Amanda didn't tell Leah what her beliefs were or that they were wrong—she simply asked questions.

You can uncover your own core beliefs in just the same way—by asking questions. Try the downward arrow technique yourself. First, try to become aware of thoughts racing around your mind, and slow down enough to put a few of them into words. Write them down if you can. Then look at these thoughts and get curious about them. Ask if you have any evidence for them, or if there may be alternative explanations.

To do the downward arrow technique, identify a thought that is distressing you. Then, ask one of the following questions of it:

What would be so bad about that?

What does that imply?

And so what?

What does that mean?

Keep asking in exactly the way Dr. Amanda did, and soon you will arrive at a core belief. The interesting thing is that people's negative core beliefs tend to be very similar—they're often variations on the theme of not being good enough, or of the world being a dangerous or bad place. Try not to get too hung up on the wording of the belief—a core belief is not a verbal thing. It's a way of making sense of the world, and it encompasses our feelings, assumptions, and ways that we make meaning.

Session 3

By the time Leah returned for the third session, she was feeling completely different. She hated to admit it to herself, but for the first time in a long time there was something a little embarrassing, a little vulnerable happening to her: She had *hope*. She doesn't know how it would look yet, but she allowed herself just the tiniest permission to hope that her sessions with Dr. Amanda just might possibly work. That this just might be a way forward for her—although she was not quite ready to let her expectations get too large, lest everything prove to be a flop after all.

She arrived at the session filled with cautious, fragile optimism. She proudly presented the completed homework pages to Dr. Amanda, who was pleased to receive them. Leah spent the first ten minutes of the session chattering excitedly.

She had mulled over last week's session and felt she had something of a breakthrough. Dr. Amanda was right; she did have a core belief that she absolutely had to get everyone to like her ... or else. And what's more, combined with the homework exercises, her newfound awareness of this core belief meant she was suddenly seeing it *everywhere* ... it really did impact her life in every way.

"I'm proud of you. I can see you've really taken these exercises and run with them. You're doing good work," said Dr. Amanda.

Leah blushed. "Well, I guess. Congratulations!" she said sardonically. "Maybe with ten more years of therapy, I can eventually just do the normal things that everyone else does without trying, right?" Leah gave a bitter laugh, but the mood in the office immediately changed. Dr. Amanda crossed and uncrossed her legs.

"Leah, when I gave you a compliment, you immediately undermined it. Did you notice that you did that?"

"I ... I was only joking, I guess."

"Were you? Seems to me you really don't agree when I said that you were doing good work."

"Well ... I mean ... gah!" Leah threw her hands up in exasperation.

"This homework you've completed for me was all about taking a closer look at some of your self-talk—the way your core beliefs shape how you think and feel about your life. I think we're seeing your core beliefs play out right now. People with low self-esteem often have a core belief that they are fundamentally worth less than other human beings."

Leah thought about this for a moment. She could see what Dr. Amanda was driving at—it was no surprise to anyone that Leah was sometimes down on herself and often very negative. But she didn't quite agree that it was because she had "low self-esteem," exactly. Leah didn't think that she was being negative—more like just being realistic!

"The thing is, I'm an *introvert*, and I'm very shy. I prefer one-on-one interactions, and I like to keep to myself. I'm a quiet person. That often means that people don't understand me, and maybe they don't like me because I'm just too different, and maybe they're threatened by that. I'm not like everyone else. I don't fit into the world and all its stupid rules. And I'm tired of trying to. Why should I always have to change? Introverts are valuable too, and it's high time society stopped undervaluing them and treating them the way they do. This is just the way I am."

Leah suddenly felt angry and didn't know where the anger was coming from. She resented Dr.

Amanda always trying to label her—"anxiety," "low self-esteem." It was so, so much more complicated than that! And Dr. Amanda herself couldn't understand that because she was just a conventional therapist who probably only worked with other unintelligent people and their boring, predictable problems. The room was quiet now, and Leah bit her lip, annoyed but not quite sure who or what the target of her annoyance was.

"Leah, I'm really glad you've shared all that with me. You seem to place a lot of value in this identity of being an introvert. It has a lot of meaning for you."

"Yes, as a matter of fact it does."

"So, to you, an introvert is someone who is quiet and shy. Someone who is different from everyone else. Someone who doesn't fit in."

"Exactly."

"And how does an introvert behave when they're in the company of other people?"

"How do they behave? Well, if they're smart, they avoid other people in the first place!"

"Why?"

"Because people are jerks. They're boring and judgmental and mean."

"So, it seems like being an introvert also means always being rejected by other people . . . as a rule."

This gave Leah pause. She couldn't quite decide whether to agree or disagree with this statement. Before she could speak, Dr. Amanda was talking again.

"Leah, sometimes people create certain rules and roles for themselves in life. They tell themselves certain stories about who they are and how they should behave to survive in the world. For some people, the story they tell is one in which they are the underdogs, the victims, or the excluded ones. They believe at their core that they are fundamentally worth less than other people. And to help protect themselves from this horrible idea, and to cope with it, they make rules and roles for themselves. So long as they follow the rules and act out the role, they can defend against this feeling of being inferior. In your case, I think that your core belief is that you are worthless. I also think that you've created this identity for yourself—the identity you call 'introvert'—which is a way to cope with that. The rule is that other people have to approve of you and like you, or else you're worthless. The rule is that other people have to validate you for you to have any value. And yet .

. ." Here she paused for a moment. "And yet you say you actually don't want to fit in, anyway, and you say the world and its rules are stupid. On the one hand, you find some worth and value in calling yourself an introvert, and you're proud of that, but on the other, you tell me that an introvert is someone who is always rejected and disliked by the world. I think something is not really holding up, is it? Perhaps this role of being an unlikable introvert isn't really serving you after all."

"You're wrong, Dr. Amanda. People have rejected me in the past *because* I'm an introvert."

"Or maybe calling yourself an introvert is a way to make it so that when people reject you, it doesn't hurt so much?"

"That doesn't even make sense . . ."

"If someone rejects you, you can tell a story that really, they are rejecting you because you're special, different—perhaps even better than they are. In fact, you can say that you almost *want* them to reject you, because then at least it's something you decided, not them."

Leah felt angrier than ever.

"You know what, I came in here this morning feeling really positive about all this. But I don't know, it's like . . . it's like you're saying that it's all my fault or something. You're not being very supportive."

"Maybe you're right. I do apologize if I've been harsh."

"You say I have low self-esteem, but then you also make it out like I'm doing it on purpose, like I actually am some kind of narcissist or something."

Dr. Amanda held up her hands. "Now, that's definitely *not* what I'm saying. But I am very curious about what's going on right now."

"Right now? I don't know. I guess I'm kind of mad at you."

"I touched a nerve, it seems. It wasn't my intention to hurt you."

Leah chewed her lip again. "To be honest, in a weird way you're actually right. I *am* proud of being an introvert, but I have to be. Because nobody else appreciates me, right? I think you might be on to something; I don't know."

"It can be difficult to take a really good hard look at our self-perceptions. At the stories we tell ourselves and tell others. In CBT we look at all these stories we tell and the rules we make for ourselves, the ones that are there to protect us from our own core beliefs. But we don't do this just to beat ourselves or make ourselves feel bad. We do it because we want to see if it's possible to have different core beliefs or live by different rules or play different roles."

Leah felt a little upset and still didn't know what to say.

"I'm not going to tell you what those beliefs or rules or roles should be, Leah," Dr. Amanda continued. "This is your life. Your therapy, your work to do. I'm just here to help you figure it out. I'm not perfect, and sometimes I make mistakes. I can see I've upset you."

Leah nodded sulkily.

"It seems crazy, I know, but sometimes people can get very used to the idea of themselves as broken or bad. They genuinely want to get better, but they have a hard time reconciling that with the image they already have of themselves—the image in which they're always broken. Do you understand what I'm saying?"

"I think so. But I don't think I've ever had another identity but this one."

The clock ticked quietly in the corner. The rest of the session passed quickly and in a blur. Dr. Amanda was aware that she had been a little hasty in rushing in with her own interpretation, and Leah had felt attacked. Yet both women were now quietly wondering how much truth there was in all that had been said and how to move the conversation on. Soon, the hour was over, and the two parted ways. Leah found herself traveling home yet again with a head full of things she had never really considered before.

Maybe Dr. Amanda was right. Maybe she had used this "introvert" label as a kind of shield . . . even a weapon at times. She kept returning to something Dr. Amanda had said: "Sometimes, people get used to playing the role of being broken." Something like that. Until today, Leah had never considered that she was playing a role at all.

But the more she thought about it, the more she saw that she had been. Since she could remember, she had played the role of the shy, sensitive one, the awkward loner who hid in the background, the misunderstood one, the black sheep. It was a strange sensation, imagining that there was a world out there in which she maybe didn't have to play this role. She was still angry at Dr. Amanda for many undefined reasons, but there was something else, too. Arising in her was a new kind of . . . curiosity.

Reflect

- The third session unfolded in an unexpected and rather confrontational way. How would you have responded to

hearing Dr. Amanda's frank and rather unflattering appraisal of the situation? Why do you think Leah responded with anger and indignation?
- What do you think needs to happen next for Leah?
- Finally, the idea of low self-esteem is everywhere these days, but what would your definition of low self-esteem be? Do you think Leah has low self-esteem?

In this third (admittedly difficult) session, Dr. Amanda explores two key elements:

- Leah's core beliefs
- The **rules** and **roles** she has developed to protect herself when confronting these core beliefs

Leah has a core belief that she is worthless or bad. Dr. Amanda believes she has constructed a set of life "rules" to help cope with this belief, i.e., that it is other people's judgments that determine her value, and that if she wants to feel good, she needs other people to judge her as good first. The converse is that if other people reject her, then it means that she really is bad. Additionally, Leah has constructed a role for herself to try to work around her negative and painful core beliefs. This role is a range of behaviors and assumptions that all together create the part of "introvert" (Leah's definition, anyway), which is someone who has a curious blend of both inferiority and superiority. This is a classic pattern: "They have rejected me ... but I don't care because I reject them first!"

Low self-esteem often looks like a poor self-image, shyness, pessimism, self-doubt, self-criticism, and approval-seeking. But it can also look like a compensatory arrogance, exaggerated confidence, or the denial of wanting or needing others' approval. A core belief that you are worthless can manifest as depression, lack of motivation, apathy and dependency, insecurity, avoidance, underachieving, withdrawal, poor communication and social skills, a tendency to quit and give up, and the unwillingness to take risks (because you're only going to fail like always, right?).

Low self-esteem, however, can also show up as failing to take responsibility for your actions, blaming others, or assuming a victim role that is not entirely warranted. Those with low self-esteem can learn unhealthy patterns of behavior, such as passive aggression or manipulation, primarily because they don't believe they are entitled to ask for what they want, or that they possess the ability to pursue it for themselves.

This is perhaps why Dr. Amanda "touched a nerve" in this session with Leah—she called out the inconsistencies in Leah's self-created role. Can you sense the tension in Leah as she tries to reconcile the fact that she considers the problem to stem from her being "shy" and an "introvert" but also does not want to abandon these labels and the sense of righteous victimhood that come with them?

In your own life, you, too, can start to consider the rules and roles that your own core beliefs have inspired you to adopt. In the grand play of life, what part are you acting out? What rules of living are you following, and what is their ultimate purpose? Some examples:

"The world is a scary and dangerous place (core belief), and that's why I have to be super-organized and responsible for everything (role). If I don't stay in control and on top of things, everything will be a disaster (rule)."

"I am worth nothing (core belief). If I want to be a good person, then I have to always be helpful and useful to other people. If I am a perfectly selfless, caring, and devoted person, then everyone will have to love me, and I will be valuable (rule and role)."

"There is something very wrong with me (core belief). I have to keep people at arm's length so nobody discovers how wrong I am and rejects me or hurts me because of it (rule). As long as I'm the cold, cruel tough guy, then people tend to stay away (role)."

Of course, when written down in this way, core beliefs, rules, and roles can all seem overly simplistic and neat. Real life is a lot messier, but it's still worth exploring the relationship between what you believe about yourself and how this impacts your behaviors and self-concept. In our hypothetical story, Leah tackles these issues head-on and quickly—in reality, working on core beliefs can require considerable time and patience!

Session 4

It was November 1st, the day after Halloween, and Dr. Amanda and Leah had just seated themselves to begin their fourth session together. The session before had felt tense and even a little dangerous . . . but now, in the warm autumn light, it was hard to ignore that a certain friendliness had appeared in the room. Leah didn't really know anything about Dr. Amanda, yet she was beginning to feel a lot more comfortable around her. It wasn't that she felt that Dr. Amanda was her friend. It was different somehow—it felt more like a kind of trust, a kind of honesty. Leah was beginning to feel like she could talk about anything with Dr. Amanda. And today, during the fourth session, she wondered just how much soul-baring she might allow herself to indulge in . . .

The two began chatting about Halloween, and Leah explained that she had gone to a party the night before, hosted by a fellow student in her course. She proudly told Dr. Amanda that even though she was hesitant, she pushed herself to wear a fancy dress costume that would definitely draw attention. This, Leah thought, was a good sign—it showed that she was challenging these things that they were beginning to uncover together, these unspoken roles she had been play-acting. It showed that she was building her self-esteem.

"Tell me more about this costume," said Dr. Amanda.

"Well, I went as a moth!"

"A *moth*?"

"Yes, it was amazing. I had this beautiful cape, you see, kind of printed with these moth wing colors, and then on my head I wore these giant antennae—fuzzy moth antennae—and I had this awesome bodysuit made out of, like, fur. You know, to make me look fuzzy."

"Wow. Sounds like a lot of work went into that costume."

"It did. I actually made it last year but never got round to wearing it. So I thought this year, I'm going to do it!"

Dr. Amanda smiled warmly.

"The thing about the costume," Leah continued, "is that to see the full effect, you have to open your arms really wide, like this." She stood up and demonstrated. "And that way you can see all these amazing colors in the wings, you know?"

"I can see how that would have grabbed attention!"

"Yeah. It really did. I also . . . this is going to sound stupid, though."

"Tell me."

"I also wore this kind of . . . silvery wig . . ."

Leah paused and peered at Dr. Amanda as though to check what she thought of this.

"Is that stupid?" she said. "Seems like wearing a wig on Halloween is exactly the right thing to do?"

"Well, yeah. But for me it wasn't easy."

"No?"

"No. I was thinking about what we were saying, about roles and core beliefs. I don't know, this wig thing was . . ." She struggled to find the words.

"What were you thinking when you put that wig on?"

Leah thought for a long time. "Honestly?"

Dr. Amanda laughed. "Of course honestly! What else are we here for, hm?"

"Well . . . honestly I felt . . . like a fake."

"Like a fake. Tell me more what you mean by that."

"Well, I don't know. When I was at home and I looked in the mirror, I thought I looked pretty good, you know? Pretty, even. I know that sounds stupid, but I think it actually looked good on me. Then when I went out, I . . ."

Dr. Amanda waited.

"I . . . just suddenly felt like a big fake."

"You no longer thought you looked pretty?"

"No, it was more like . . . I thought I did look pretty."

"So, what's the problem?"

"The problem is . . ." Leah sighed. It was so hard to put her thoughts and feelings into words. "I felt as though I was a fake for trying to act pretty. Like, usually I'm just the kind of plain girl, you know? Like, I'm not beautiful—I'm okay with that. But then there I was, trying to act all pretty . . ."

"Where you *acting* pretty or did you actually look pretty?"

This question genuinely confused Leah.

"I think . . . I think that everyone else was looking at me and thinking that I was pathetic, that I was just vain and looking for attention. I don't know . . . like it was embarrassing that people could tell that I was trying to look nice. Does that make sense?"

"It does."

"I think they must have pitied me a little, seeing me make all that effort."

"Who are these *they*? Who are we talking about?"

"Well, you know, people. Everybody."

"But who?"

"Well, the people I went with. There was a crowd of about ten of us. We all went together."

"All ten of these people told you that they pitied you? That they thought you were vain and pathetic?"

"No, they didn't say that, obviously. But... I could tell."

"Leah, do you think this perception of yourself as vain and all that... do you think that's something that's going on out there, with those people, or something happening here, with *you*? In your mind?"

Leah squirmed in her chair. "I know what you're saying, Dr. Amanda, I really do. But there were some things. This guy Dan kind of looked me up and down with a really weird look on his face. Nobody said anything nice about my costume, at all. And then later someone made a joke about how we were all drama queens."

"And you thought that joke was about you?"

Now that she had said it, Leah felt that perhaps this little detail was exaggerated.

"Okay, maybe the joke wasn't about me. But . . ."

"You said you've been thinking about your core belief, about your roles and rules. Can you remind me of the core belief we discovered?"

"Yeah. It was . . . that other people don't like me. That I'm a bad person. Something like that."

"So, I have a question for you."

"Okay."

"Imagine there was a really bad person . . . help me quickly think of an example of a bad person."

"I don't know . . . a murderer?"

"Yes, a murderer. Let's imagine a serial killer—a really *bad* person, right? Now the serial killer decides one day to dress up like, I don't know, Jesus. Like an angel with wings and a halo. What do you think of him now?"

"I think . . . he's being deceptive. He's dressing up as someone he isn't. Wait! Is that what you're saying about me? That I was dressing up as someone I wasn't?"

"Well, I'm actually saying something a little different—that you were dressing up as someone you *perceived* as very different from who you really are. When you put the wig on, you said it was pretty, right?"

"Yes."

"And from the sounds of it, the costume was really beautiful."

"It was."

"And yet you say that when you put those things on, you felt like a fake. So, if these things are pretty and beautiful, and you're a fake wearing them, what does that mean about you?"

"It means . . . well, it means that I'm *not* pretty. I see what you mean."

"You felt uncomfortable."

"You mean I felt uncomfortable because being pretty was like wearing a costume that didn't fit?"

"I'm saying that if you perceive yourself as bad, unworthy, or ugly, then when you act and behave like someone who isn't those things, then it feels kinda . . ." Dr. Amanda paused so Leah would finish the sentence for her.

"Fake," said Leah, nodding. "It feels all wrong and fake."

"Exactly."

"So, it's what you were saying last time. That I'm playing this kind of role..."

"Perhaps at the Halloween party last night, you experimented a little with being outside that role."

"It felt . . . weird. But I really did love that costume."

"I'm sure you did. But maybe in the back of your mind, you were saying something like, *This isn't like you. This isn't something that a person like you ever does.*"

"Yeah, that's exactly what it was like," said Leah.

"If you really thought that way, if you thought that you were actually a bad and ugly person who was just in a disguise, then when you went out into the world, what do you think you would find there?"

"What do you mean?"

"Well, that boy you mentioned, Dan? He looked you up and down, you said."

"Yeah. I felt so embarrassed."

"What do you think *he* was thinking?"

"He was thinking . . . she's such a fake. She's a poser trying to be someone she's not."

"And yet, he didn't actually say those words."

"No."

"So where did those words come from? He didn't say them. So, who did say them?"

Leah smiled. "Me, I guess. I said them in my head."

"So, it seems like, when you think *I'm a fake*, then when you go into the world, you discover a lot of people who agree with you!"

"Yeah . . . I guess so."

"Here's something in the world—this guy Dan looking at you—and you interpret it in a particular way. But you don't interpret it neutrally. You interpret it according to what you already believe to be true. And what do you already believe to be true?"

"That I'm bad? That I'm ugly?"

"To a person who thinks they're bad, a look can feel like judgment. But picture someone who already believes that they're fantastic, that they're beautiful. What do you think such a person would assume if someone looked at *them*?"

"They'd think . . . they'd think that everyone was admiring them and thinking how great they looked."

"Right. You're doing the same thing. None of us really perceives reality exactly as it is. We perceive things through our own filters, and we interpret them *through* that filter. We look at things and decide what they mean according to what we have already concluded about ourselves, about the world."

"Yes, I totally get that. I have a friend—Gemma. She's just like you say. She thinks she's fat, and of course she's not. She's actually super skinny. It's so annoying. But she completely refuses to listen to anyone who tells her that. It's like she becomes deaf or something. You could just argue with her forever about it; she won't believe anything other than that she's fat, end of story. Once I asked her, why does everyone say that you're *not* fat, then? How come nobody has ever called you fat? Do you know what her answer was? She said that everyone secretly thought she was fat and felt bad for her, so they deliberately went out of their way to say the opposite so they didn't hurt her feelings. That's crazy!"

Dr. Amanda laughed. "That is crazy. But tell me why it's crazy."

"Well . . . it's like, even when something is proof right there in front of her eyes, it's like she deliberately chooses to twist it around and to take it to mean the opposite of what it actually means."

"Sounds like you're on to something. Do you think you did a little of that yourself yesterday, at the Halloween party?"

"Well . . . maybe . . . but not as bad as Gemma." Leah smiled.

"If you were trying to get Gemma to see that she wasn't fat, what would you do, do you think?"

Leah sighed. "I have no idea. Just telling her does nothing."

"I agree. If I were just to *tell* you that you weren't bad, weren't ugly, and so on, would you believe me?"

Leah contemplated this. Both her and Dr. Amanda already knew the answer.

"It's like, I do understand it. I do agree with you, and I can see how it plays out in Gemma's life. I think everything you're saying is right. It's just . . . I don't *feel* it."

"Leah, I think you're touching on something very important here. You know, in CBT it's not just about sitting and having a discussion. It's not about me just convincing you intellectually of some idea and informing you of the right way to think and feel. Because, as you've already told me, it doesn't mean anything until you actually feel that for yourself. It's not just about feeling; it's about your core belief. I call them core beliefs because these are not just passing thoughts that pop in and out of your head—these are deep, long-lasting ideas that have been with us sometimes for life."

"You know, Dr. Amanda, I was thinking that maybe all this comes from childhood. My mom always said stuff like this, you know? She always told me to stop showing off, to stop trying to get attention. Do you think that's where it comes from?"

"Maybe," said Dr. Amanda. "But tell me something. If I said right now that yes, your core belief about yourself comes from your mother and from your early childhood, if I agreed with you and said that that was the explanation, does that suddenly change your core belief? Does it make it easier to immediately think about things differently?"

"No. Not really."

"That's what I'm getting at. Changing them is not just a matter of insight or of understanding why things are the way they are. It's not just a question of knowing what's 'right' and then changing our minds."

"So how do we change them, then?" Leah said, her voice a little despairing. What was the point of therapy if talking couldn't change your mind?!

Dr. Amanda looked at her clock. Frustratingly, there were just a few minutes left.

"Leah, before you go, I want to tell you a little story. Is that okay?"

"Yeah."

"Okay, well, here it is: There once was a man who was absolutely terrified of elephants, right? Deathly afraid of them. When he was a kid, he saw in a cartoon that elephants were afraid of mice. So, he decided that what he'd do is keep a little mouse with him at all times in his pocket to scare away any elephants. Never mind that there are no elephants where he lives, and also even if there were, they wouldn't exactly be out to get him. Also, it's just a myth that elephants are afraid of mice—they're not really. But now let's say you see this guy walking around town with his mouse in his pocket. You tell him that the mouse won't help him, that he doesn't need it. He tells you, 'I haven't been attacked by an elephant yet, have I? So, it must be working!' Now what are you going to say to him to convince him that this idea he has is wrong, that the mouse is not helping him?"

"You can't just explain it to him," Leah said.

"Probably not. So, this week, I want you to think carefully about how you would get this man to overcome his rules about himself and about how the world works. Then tell me at our next session. Deal?"

"Okay. Deal."

Reflect

- How would you answer the question that Dr. Amanda poses at the end of this session?
- Why do you think Dr. Amanda has told Leah this story, and what do you make of it?
- "I was thinking that maybe all this comes from childhood. My mom always said stuff like this, you know? She always told me to stop showing off, to stop trying to get attention. Do you think that's where it comes from?" Leah is wondering whether her self-concept has been influenced by her early childhood experiences. What do you think?

Our core beliefs may indeed be formed in early life, where we internalize other people's perceptions and make them our own. Nevertheless, it is *we* who maintain that core belief in the present, and we do that by engaging in self-talk that reinforces all those rules and assumptions about who we are, what we are capable of, and what the world is like.

Leah is gradually learning that her *interpretation* of reality is not necessarily the same as reality itself. She is beginning to see that her perception of reality is not neutral but distorted, and the meaning she makes of events around her is organized around a central concept—her idea of who she is and how other people perceive her. This can be a strange place to be in mentally.

Many of us will point to outside events and other people as the source of our problems, not noticing how much of what we attribute to them is really originating within us.

This is the paradox of genuine change—we may want with all our hearts to be different, but we still carry the inertia of all our old past patterns and habitual ways of doing things. Like Leah, we step out of our comfort zone and discover that, well, it's uncomfortable!

As you think about your own self-perception and how it may be influenced by your core beliefs, try answering the following questions:

- How do I see myself fundamentally? Complete the sentence, *I am a* _____.
- How do I believe other people see me? What am I using to reach these conclusions?
- How might my sense of self be stemming from my core beliefs?
- Who decides what kind of person I am? Me or other people? Both?

Session 5

"I think I have an answer for you."

"I can't wait to hear it," said Dr. Amanda.

"What I would tell this guy, the guy who was afraid of elephants, is that he'd have to trust me and let me take the mouse away from him, just for a short time, so that he could see that no elephants attacked him, and then he'd prove to himself that it wasn't the mouse keeping them away at all."

"That sounds like a smart thing to do. Sounds a bit like . . . an experiment?"

"Yeah, exactly. I'd tell him, 'Let's test it.' Let's see if this mouse is really doing anything for you. If we take it away and no elephants come, then we have proper evidence that you're safe and that you don't need this mouse anymore."

"You're really getting it, Leah. And I'm sure you can see why I told you that little story."

"Well . . . that's what I'm not perfectly clear on, actually. I'm trying to understand what I have in common with this guy."

"Well, maybe you have a mouse too. I think we all have our own version of the mouse."

"What's my mouse, then?"

"Well, let's think about it. In the story, why does the man keep the mouse?"

"He keeps it because he thinks it will help him stay safe."

"Exactly. We all have beliefs like that—the rules and roles I told you about—that we carry around with us because, in one way or another, we believe that they will protect us. Keep us safe. The mouse is really just a set of beliefs. Of ideas."

"So . . . I have ideas and beliefs that I carry with me that I use to keep me safe . . ."

"I wonder what they could be? I think we spoke about it already once before."

"You mean my core belief? The role I play? But I don't understand. If I see myself as a bad person, if I see myself as an introvert and all that, then . . . well, *that* doesn't keep me safe!"

"Doesn't it? Remind me what you do—what actions you take—when you believe that you're inferior and bad and different."

"Um . . . I guess I said that I don't do much of anything. I hide away."

"Why hide away?"

"Well . . . because like I said, people are mean. People judge you."

"Aha. So, I can see something you might like to protect yourself from."

"So, you're saying . . . if I hide away and don't do anything, then that means I'll protect myself?"

"Maybe. What might you want to protect yourself from?"

"Other people judging me."

"Exactly. In one of our early sessions, we uncovered that core belief—*if people don't like me, it means I'm a bad person*. If you hide away, though, then people can't judge you. So, you're safe."

Leah stewed over this for a moment.

"I guess that does make sense. So, my mouse is . . . this idea that I have to hide away."

"I can think of a word that you've used before to describe exactly that kind of person . . ."

"*Introvert*! You mean introvert, don't you?"

Dr. Amanda laughed.

"So, you're telling me . . . that my mouse is the idea I have of myself . . . the idea that I'm an introvert?"

"Well, I'm not telling you anything, Leah. We already said there's no point in me just telling you stuff, right? But I have been wondering about it myself, and now I want to see what you make of it."

Leah didn't respond for a while, and the clock ticked away a second at a time, never altering its rhythm.

"Dr. Amanda, do you think that someone can give you a mouse? Like can you inherit one?"

Dr. Amanda tilted her head to the side. "That sounds interesting. What do you mean?"

"I told you last time that my mother was really critical of me growing up. I haven't . . . mentioned her to you yet. It's weird that we're in our fifth session and I haven't even told you about her."

"Is there something you feel I should know?"

Leah's face suddenly fell.

"My mom was . . . she was really difficult. She passed away a few years ago . . ." She quickly scanned Dr. Amanda's face. Nothing. "But before she passed away, we didn't exactly have a good relationship, anyway. She was just . . . she was a real bitch, actually! Nothing I did was good enough for her. Thinking about it now, I'm pretty sure she was abusive, you know? Emotionally abusive. I think she's a big part of the reason I am the way I am—"

Dr. Amanda immediately interrupted. "The way you are?"

"Yeah, you know. Shy and with low self-esteem and everything. I think that because she criticized me growing up, I kind of carried that with me. Like you say, like a mouse. Like she gave it to me."

"I see."

"Do you think that's what happened? Do you think that's the root cause of all this?"

Dr. Amanda sighed and adjusted herself in her seat and took her time before answering.

"There's something I always tell my clients, Leah, and it's this: A vicious cycle has no root. Maybe something started with your mom; maybe it didn't. But my question to you is, what's *maintaining* things? You say 'the way you are.' Well, what are you doing every day—what are you doing right now—to maintain that?"

"What am I doing? Well, I'm having all these thoughts, this trauma and all that, and I'm carrying it with me . . ."

"Okay, so if I tell the man with the mouse that it was his mom who originally gave him the mouse, and told him to put it in his pocket . . . is that it? Will that solve the problem?"

"Probably not."

"Look, Leah, I'll be honest. Lots of people come to therapy expecting that there's going to be a lot of digging around in the past and exploring old childhood trauma and wounds and stuff like that. But I think you can see why that's not always helpful. The real question is, who put that mouse in the man's pocket *today*?"

"He did?"

"And who has the power to take the mouse out right now?"

"He does," said Leah.

"Exactly. It can be interesting to find out how the mouse got there in the first place. But if we want to make changes, we have to see why the mouse *continues* to stay in his pocket."

"It stays there because he keeps choosing to keep it there; that's what you're saying."

"Yeah. Look, maybe eventually he just does it out of habit. He just does it because he's always done it. But as you told me at the beginning of this session, one way to start making changes is to *test it*—test this idea that he *needs* the mouse.

And you can only do that by taking the mouse away and seeing what happens."

Leah nodded thoughtfully.

"How do I do that for myself? How do I do an experiment on my own ideas?"

"Well, let's see. You have a core belief that you're a bad person, that you're unworthy, right?"

"Yeah."

"And so, you have a rule that you must never put yourself out there, because if you do, people will judge you, and that means that you really will be a bad person. So, to stay safe, you have to hide. Now, if I were challenging this, I'd try to do the *opposite*. What's the opposite of hiding away?"

"It's . . ." Leah thought for a second. "It's putting yourself out there, like you say. It's making yourself known. Being visible."

"Like . . . wearing a cute silver wig?"

Leah laughed. "Yeah, like that."

"So, what would you say about doing an experiment where you deliberately try to do the opposite of what you'd normally do, to prove to yourself that this idea—this idea that you're just a bad introvert and an unlikeable person—isn't helping you and it isn't even true?"

"Okay, but how?"

"Well, you tell me. What would be a pretty scary thing to do? What kind of thing would make you *most visible* and have lots and lots of people looking at you?"

"Hmm . . . I don't know. The wig was like that, I guess."

"Okay, what if you wore your silver wig in a tutorial one day?"

"Oh my God, what?! You have to be joking." Leah laughed.

"Okay, okay, I hear you. That's pretty extreme. Let's call the wig in class a ten on the scary scale. What would be, like, a five for you?"

"Umm . . . well, I suppose that would be something like me talking in a tutorial, asking lots of questions, stuff like that."

"Okay, that's good. What do you think would happen if you did this in your next tutorial?"

Leah's eyes went wide. "I don't know. People would probably think I'm an idiot. They'd think I'm weird for suddenly speaking up. Maybe they'd laugh at me."

"Okay. What I want you to do is write all that down. That's a prediction, okay? Then you're going to actually try speaking up in class, for real, and come back and tell me what happens. But be like a scientist when you do it. You've got your hypothesis, you'll gather data, and you'll bring it back to me and we'll have a look at it. We'll analyze it and see what conclusions we can draw. How does that sound?"

For the next fifteen minutes, Dr. Amanda and Leah carefully made a plan for exactly what Leah would do in her next tutorial class, which was just two days away. They agreed together on a plan of action and wrote it down. Leah felt terrified. But she also felt a little excited. It was almost like a game.

"Oh man, I'm going to make such a fool of myself. I can't believe I'm going to do this." Leah laughed. "I'm going to come back and tell you a huge disaster story, just watch."

"Well, fine, that's the prediction. I'm going to wait and see," said Dr. Amanda.

"Okay, I know you say that, but this will be interesting, you'll see. People really *will* laugh at me."

"But why should they?"

"I don't know. Because I'm awkward. I open my mouth and just sound like an idiot."

"Leah, would you say what you just said—you're awkward and an idiot—to a good friend of yours?"

"Well, I would. If they were being awkward and an idiot, I guess."

Dr. Amanda smiled.

"Okay, let's try this. We have a few minutes left—would you do a little exercise with me?"

As Leah nodded, Dr. Amanda stood and arranged a few of the chairs in the office in a triangle. She invited Leah to stand and did the same.

"See these chairs, Leah? Each of them represents a different part of yourself. There are three parts—let's call this one here the *criticizer*, this one in the corner the *criticized*, and that one over there the *compassionate observer*. Got it?"

"Criticizer, criticized, compassionate observer. Okay," said Leah as she pointed to each chair.

Dr. Amanda guided Leah to sit in the criticizer chair.

"Can you repeat what you just said?"

"What, about me being awkward and speaking like an idiot?"

"Exactly. But throw a whole bunch more stuff in there, if you like. That's the criticizer chair, so, you know, criticize away."

Leah smiled. She loved doing games like this in the office, even though she wouldn't admit to Dr. Amanda that they were truly her favorite part of every session.

"Okay. Well, I'm awkward. I sound like an idiot when—"

"No, no. Say it in second person—say you're awkward and so on. You're not Leah now; you're just the criticizer."

"Uh, okay. *You're* awkward. Whenever you open your mouth to speak, you sound like an idiot. Um . . . you always embarrass yourself. Actually, you're a bit of a loser, if I'm honest."

"Anything else?"

"Well, yeah, actually. Like, why can't you just figure this stuff out already? Everyone else your age has learned how to get their lives together, and you're still moping around like a baby, having to go to therapy like some crybaby. Seriously. What makes you think you're so special that you need therapy all the time? It's pretty stupid."

"Great!" said Dr. Amanda. "Ready to switch chairs now?" She gestured toward the chair for the criticized. Leah hesitated. It felt bad to suddenly put herself in the line of fire.

"I . . . I . . . I'm sorry, I guess. It's true. I am awkward, but . . . well, it's not my fault, okay? Why does everyone want me to be someone I'm not? I'm *sorry* I'm such a loser, okay? I hate myself too, if that means anything. I don't know what to say."

"How do you feel right now?" Dr. Amanda asked.

Leah shrugged. "Like crap."

"Do you feel like talking to people? Sharing your opinion? Asking questions? Socializing?"

"No. Jesus. I feel like crawling into a hole and dying."

"Come and sit in the other chair now."

Leah dragged herself off the chair and sat in the compassionate observer chair.

"Okay. Whenever you're ready."

"What am I supposed to say now?" Leah said, wide-eyed.

"Well, this chair is for the part of you that is kind and understanding. A wise part of you that only wants the best for you."

Leah blinked. For the longest time, she couldn't think of a single thing to say. This struck her immediately. Did this mean that she didn't have a wise, kind part of her? Was it really the case that she never spoke to herself with compassion? There was no denying it—insulting herself had come easy. But when asked to speak to herself kindly, she was genuinely stumped.

"You . . . you're okay," she eventually stammered. "I know you're doing your best . . ." It felt like a mammoth effort to say those few words.

"Go on."

"You're not a loser. You're having a hard time, and it's okay to have a hard time. You can . . . learn to be more sociable if you want. But it's not as bad as you say."

Without saying a word, Dr. Amanda patted the criticized chair again, and Leah went to sit there once more. This time, Leah knew what to do.

"Thank you," she said emphatically. "Thank you for saying that. It . . . means a lot."

"How do you feel now? When that wise part of you speaks to you with kindness and understanding?"

"I feel . . . well things don't feel quite so terrible. I mean, like I can deal with it. Like it's okay to be struggling a little bit."

"Do you think, the way you feel now, you could talk with someone, share your opinion, put yourself out there?"

"It would still be scary," Leah said. "But I guess it would feel a little easier . . ."

Dr. Amanda put the chairs back in their original position.

"Tell me what you've just taught yourself," she said, and Leah smiled.

Reflect

- What do you think of Dr. Amanda's mouse story? Do you yourself have any ideas, beliefs, or habits that you carry around

with you in the unconscious hope that they will protect you from something?
- At one point in the session, Leah is keen to discuss her childhood, and especially her mother's criticism of her and how that may have impacted her self-esteem. But Dr. Amanda doesn't follow this path. Do you agree with her that there's no point "dwelling on the past"? Or do you think it would help Leah explore where her negative core beliefs came from originally?
- Dr. Amanda and Leah together decide on an "experiment" for Leah to do in two days' time. What do you predict might be an obstacle to Leah running the experiment completely, and what do you expect will happen if she does muster up the courage to speak in her next tutorial class?

You can try your own version of the "criticizer, criticized, and compassionate observer" exercise. This technique was inspired by Leslie Greenberg, a Gestalt therapist who expanded on the well-known two-chair technique, where clients are encouraged to manifest the relationship between certain aspects of themselves and others by play-acting a dialogue using two chairs.

This version is great for revealing the nature of our own inner conflicts—when we criticize ourselves, there is, of course, a part that we are criticizing. But there is also another part that would defend and protect that more vulnerable aspect and argue against the mean and sometimes irrational criticisms coming from the criticizer.

This exercise is not just about words, however. Dr. Amanda asks Leah how she feels inhabiting each of these chairs/mindsets. She also draws her attention to the fact that certain actions may feel more natural in one chair but completely impossible in another. This again is the essence of CBT—our actions and feelings are directly related to the thoughts and beliefs we hold. For Leah, being in self-critical mode makes her feel like "crap" but also discourages her from connecting with her world, from speaking up, from taking risks, and from sharing her opinion. We can see, in other words, where her role and identity as an awkward introvert comes from— a blend of her own self-criticism and her desire to defend against this: "It's true. I am awkward, but . . . well, it's not my fault, okay? Why does everyone want me to be someone I'm not? I'm *sorry* I'm such a loser, okay?"

Leah discovers something interesting: that it's easier to criticize herself than to stand up for herself. In other words, she has a well-established habit of being mean to herself! It will take practice to develop that inner compassionate voice and strengthen it so it can start to really argue against her automatic tendency to undermine and insult herself.

You can try your own version of this exercise by using a journal and simply writing down your thoughts and feelings from each perspective. If you can, however, it's worth getting up and sitting in different seats. The literal switch in perspective can really help drive home the shift in attitude and mental frame and show you that you are inhabiting a very particular (biased) frame of mind. Ask yourself the same question Dr. Amanda asks Leah: What lesson can you teach yourself? There is a wise, kind part inside you, even if it's been silent for some time. What does it have to say?

Session 6

On the sixth session, Leah started chatting comfortably with Dr. Amanda, expressing how fast the time had gone and how surprised she had been by all the twists and turns. Initially, she had thought three sessions would be on the long side, but now she felt like they were just getting started, and could easily imagine them doing at least ten together.

"Before you go on and I forget," said Dr. Amanda, "did you complete the homework? Or as I should say, conduct the experiment?"

"Oh. That." Leah looked out the window.

"How did it go?"

"Well . . . I was waiting for you to ask. It's weird, actually."

"Wait, before you tell me what result you got, I want to remind myself of the prediction you made . . . the hypothesis." Dr. Amanda pulled out some notes from the session before, pushed her glasses up the bridge of her nose, and read out loud. *I'm going to make a fool of myself. People will laugh at me. I'll come back and tell Dr. Amanda that the whole thing was a disaster.* Do you remember that we wrote this down together?"

Leah nodded but bit her lip.

"The thing is, Dr. Amanda, I'll admit that that didn't happen. Maybe..."

"Maybe...?"

"Maybe my prediction was wrong, I'll give you that. But..."

"Tell me what happened."

"Well, it's like we agreed. I went to my tutorial. About twenty minutes in, the guy starts asking some questions, we're, like, making a mind map, and I speak up and share this little idea I had. Actually, I was directly disagreeing with this other guy who always talks in class. I just came out and gave my own opinion—a different opinion."

"And?"

"The tutor wrote it up on the board."

"Did they laugh at you?"

"Nah."

"Was it a disaster?"

"No, it wasn't. In fact . . . nothing happened at all, really. It was weird."

"Why was it weird?"

"I expected them to say *something* . . . but they just sort of moved on. In fact, I spoke up again later on, and the same thing happened."

"They ignored you?"

"No, not at all. It was just kind of . . . uneventful."

"Seems like you're almost disappointed that things didn't catch fire or something." Dr. Amanda laughed.

"I mean . . . kinda. It was sort of like not a bad outcome but not a good one, either."

"So, you spoke up in class and, well, nothing really happened? No mockery, no congratulations."

"You know what I think, Dr. Amanda? I think people were really just caught up in their own stuff. I mean, they did listen to me. They put my point on the board. Like, I actually did take part in the conversation, but I guess the whole thing just felt . . . normal."

"Normal."

Dr. Amanda sat back in her chair.

"You predicted that people would somehow penalize you for putting yourself out there. They didn't do that."

"No."

"They didn't behave as though they thought, 'Oh, here comes Leah. She's such a weirdo introvert. We all wish she would shut up.'"

"No."

"So, who *does* think that, then?"

"Yeah, I know. It's me. They clearly don't even care if I speak or not, to be honest."

"Well, when you're in a tutorial, are *you* carefully monitoring everyone, instantly deciding who's an idiot and who's not, gearing yourself up to laugh at anyone who says something you don't agree with?"

"No, of course not. I'm . . . I'm too busy worrying they're going to do that to me!"

Dr. Amanda tapped the notes in her lap. "I think today we've discovered evidence that maybe the way you're thinking about things, about yourself, is not perfectly accurate."

"Yeah. Now I've got nobody to blame!" Leah laughed, but then considered that it wasn't really much of a joke. How often had she failed to speak up in situations like that, censored herself, hidden away, absolutely convinced that she would be victimized the second she revealed herself? For a moment, she felt a pang of regret—how often had she bit her tongue? Maybe none of it had been necessary. Maybe all this time she could have been chatting away happily. *Oh God*, she thought to herself. This was exactly what Dr. Amanda had been talking about. This was what it felt like to have your mouse taken away from you.

The rest of the session, the pair tackled the worksheets that Dr. Amanda had provided, except this time, Leah didn't think they were so "simple" as they had first appeared. She felt she was beginning to really understand the value of the exercises Dr. Amanda had been pushing. The whole point, she saw now, was to make all those *invisible* thoughts and beliefs she carried out *visible* at last ... and then put them through their paces. She had felt at first that hunting out "irrational" beliefs this way was a kind of *gotcha!*—something to catch her out. But now, she was taking a kind of pleasure in identifying where her own thinking could be better—not because she was judging how she thought currently, but because she'd had a taste of just how good it felt to let go of a belief that really wasn't helping her.

Soon it was Leah walking Dr. Amanda through all the steps of the process. She was getting better at it, too. She'd pause and become aware. She'd notice a particularly habitual thought or idea she'd had, and then she became curious about it. Then, like the scientist she always had been at heart, she began to dig around for alternate explanations. Different interpretations. Evidence for and evidence against. She was continually surprised by how often she automatically behaved as though the things she told herself mentally were one hundred percent absolute, objective fact. Really, when she slowed down and put things on paper, it started to seem like most of what was churning around inside her mind was just... *stuff*.

Just nonsense that, when it came to it, she couldn't really justify or support with cold hard evidence. So why had she been so willing to give all her mental energy and attention to something that was as good as nothing, as a story, as just something someone made up?

Once she had worked through this process herself, Dr. Amanda would repeatedly ask, "Given all this new evidence you're considering—or lack thereof—is there a better way of thinking about this situation? Of *feeling* about it?"

At first, Leah resented the implication that she could simply choose how she felt about things—surely she couldn't just snap her fingers and decide on a whim what she would and wouldn't feel? But the truth was, she caught herself more than once consciously choosing to feel hurt or ignored or abandoned or angry and so on and so on. Deliberately choosing to interpret a neutral situation so that it upset her *was* a way to choose to be upset. It was a revelation—at least some of the time, choosing how she would feel was exactly what she was doing.

Gradually, first without her noticing it, Leah's self-concept was changing. In the first session, she had proudly, angrily told Dr. Amanda that she was an "introvert" and that was just the way she was and always would be. Now, she was beginning to see just how much this identity was something she was actively *doing*. Leah had incredibly low self-worth. She was beginning to realize that this low opinion of herself had been with her for such a long time that she had begun to confuse it with her personality—even a part of her personality worth defending!

She had been trapped in a series of self-defeating behaviors that she was unable to take responsibility for, instead choosing to project them onto others and falsely imagine that *they* were the ones judging, condemning, and excluding her. Leah's experiment was the beginning of her challenging these long-held assumptions—and it would be the first in a long line of similar experiments.

As she talked with Dr. Amanda, she was more and more able to take on the voice and the mindset of that "compassionate observer" who wasn't always so quick to criticize, but who genuinely wanted what was best for her. She gently started to shift some of her beliefs about herself. She began to think that maybe she wasn't quite an "introvert," but rather that, in certain circumstances, she actually liked talking to people, expressing herself, and socializing. Rather than automatically assuming that everyone around her was breezing through life, ready to judge and reject her at the drop of a hat, she began to see that they were a lot like her—imperfect, sometimes struggling, and largely concerned with their own flaws, rather than the flaws of others.

"Dr. Amanda, can I share something with you?"

"Of course."

"When I first started coming to see you, I honestly thought the whole therapy thing was . . . stupid."

"I know."

"Yeah, but . . . I wanted to say that . . . I don't know. Thank you."

"Well, you are most welcome, Leah. But you speak as though you're saying goodbye. Are you thinking of bringing things to an end?"

Leah paused. *Was* she thinking of that? She had been feeling so much better lately, and what more was there to say? She'd had six sessions, and she had learned so much already.

"Maybe . . . maybe we do one or two more? Is that okay?"

"As I've told you already, Leah, we're not here for me. This is your space."

"But what do *you* think?"

Dr. Amanda closed her notebook and smoothed down her lap.

"What I think is not important. I can't tell you what to do. But I *do* notice that you're asking me. And that you're unsure. Why don't you think about it and we'll talk it over in the next session?"

The pair parted ways, and Leah thought about it on the way home. On the one hand, clearly Dr. Amanda was helping her. But did that mean that she should stay on and do even more, or did that mean she was "better" now and should quit? She didn't want to be in therapy forever, but on the other hand, she was really beginning to like Dr. Amanda and knowing that she was always there.

Reflect

- If you were in Leah's shoes, would you consider continuing with therapy or not? Why?
- Many CBT therapists say that their main goal is to get every client to become their own therapist. What do you think of

> Leah's ability to be her own therapist in this way?
> - CBT is not a holy grail, and the approach does have limitations. What do you think the limits of CBT are in Leah's case? Do you think it's enough to simply "challenge" thoughts and replace them with better ones?

The process of "cognitive restructuring" in CBT is not something that happens overnight but is rather something ongoing. As we've seen, because thoughts, behaviors, and feelings are all connected, it takes time for a change in one area to reflect and ripple through in the other areas. If, for example, Leah starts to really internalize the idea that she does enjoy some kinds of socializing, then that would instigate many changes in the way she acts and the way she feels about life, other people, and herself. There will, to say the least, be a few "growing pains" as this updated thought works its way through her life.

The same process can be achieved without a therapist, however, and it comes down to taking the time to answer a few key questions of any persistent thought or belief that follows you around:

- If a friend held this belief or thought this thought, what would you think? What would you tell them?

- What facts or evidence do you actually have about this situation? Is what you're thinking a fact or is it, at least in part, an opinion or interpretation?
- Are there any alternative explanations and interpretations?
- Have there ever been times when something you believed in wholeheartedly proved to be incorrect in the end?
- Even if what you're thinking and believing is "true," is it balanced, kind, useful, or necessary? Is it helping you think this way?
- If I were to zoom out and be a completely dispassionate neutral observer, what would I make of this situation?
- Given my values and principles, given my goals, and given the kind of person I would most like to be, what action can I take right now? Does this thought or belief bring me closer to the things I truly care about, or further away from them?

Session 7

When Leah walked into her seventh session with Dr. Amanda, she was sullen and withdrawn. Dr. Amanda greeted her with friendly curiosity . . . and Leah instantly burst into tears. It was a good five minutes and a dozen tissues before Leah could gather herself again, and, snuffling, explain why she was so upset.

"It's all . . . it's all gone to hell, and I'm so, so done with it all," she said, eyes red. She continued on, but Dr. Amanda had to interrupt.

"Leah, Leah, slow down. Just tell me what's happened. Last week when I saw you, you were telling me you felt ready to stop therapy because you had made so much progress. And now you're clearly very upset. What's happened between then and now?"

Leah sulked and stared at the floor. "Well, I'll tell you what's happened. You can take out that paper of yours with all my predictions written on it. Because it turns out I actually was right all along."

"You were?"

Leah blew her nose.

"It's so embarrassing. They laughed at me, okay? You promised they wouldn't, and lo and behold they did. We were giving an end-of-term presentation, and I slipped and fell. I mean, I *really* slipped. I actually hurt myself pretty badly. And these two girls in the front totally just laughed at me. I was humiliated. I wanted to just die. They saw how upset I was, and one of them said . . . I can't even tell you what they said, I'm so embarrassed."

Dr. Amanda was stunned. "Leah, I'm so sorry to hear this. That sounds really difficult. You said you hurt yourself. Are you okay now?"

"Well, my ego's pretty bashed up, but other than that, whatever."

"Leah," Dr. Amanda said eventually, "I didn't promise you that they wouldn't laugh."

There was a harsh, icy silence in the office.

"Whatever," Leah eventually repeated. "It doesn't matter now. I'm done with it, anyway."

"Done with what?"

"All of it, everything. Therapy. That stupid class. I don't care anymore."

Again, the silence.

"I can see this has really shaken you up," said Dr. Amanda, carefully trying to choose her next words.

"Everything was going fine. And then those two girls . . . ugh, I *hate* them."

"Leah, you told me to look at my paper again and revisit all those predictions you made, all the work we did on your core beliefs, your rules, your roles, all of that. I could certainly dig those up for us, but to tell you the truth . . . I don't see that anything's changed."

"What? *Everything's* changed."

"Oh? So all those awful thoughts about yourself, the ones you so successfully challenged before—none of that counts anymore?"

Leah said nothing.

"Last session, you were telling me that you were beginning to enjoy speaking up in class, and you were practicing talking to yourself with compassion, remember? I think you were really enjoying some of that."

"Yeah, but none of it worked."

"What do you mean, *worked*?"

"I mean, people were still mean to me. The thing I was worried about actually did happen after all!"

"Leah . . . is that what we were doing? Making sure that nobody ever treated you poorly ever again?"

Again, Leah could do nothing but scowl at the floor.

"Leah, let me tell you something. You have a long, old core belief that you're fundamentally not good enough. We spoke about this. A lot. We talked about how you believe that if other people reject you, it means that you're bad, remember that? We challenged that belief. And here it is again. We were making progress. You were brave enough to start challenging that core belief. But Leah, I want you to understand—our work here is to develop your self-acceptance, to have a belief in your self-worth *independent of what happens out there in the world*. This is what self-worth is. It's knowing that we have value and worth as human beings no matter what. Our goal was never to get other people to like you—after all, that would just be more of the same, right? More of the same old belief that to be good, you have to have others tell you that you're good. Do you understand what I'm saying, Leah?"

Leah was crying. She had felt so optimistic, so positive about everything. And now she felt like a fool.

"So what, I just have to keep putting myself out there for others to hurt me? Is that the point? Because that seems really unfair to me."

"Leah . . . therapy goes like this sometimes. It's easy for a while, and you make progress. And then you hit some really difficult patch. It's like a sore spot or a bruise—it hurts like hell just to touch it. But you know, those parts of therapy are valuable too. Maybe even more valuable."

"I hate all this. This shouldn't be this hard."

"Shouldn't it? What should it be like?"

"I don't know . . . like it was last time."

"Last time . . . yes, you felt strong and invulnerable then, I remember. It was so good to see you thriving like that. But the way you feel now, Leah, this hurt and disappointment—we can accept that too."

"*Accept* it? I thought the whole point was to change all the broken parts of me!"

"This feeling you have right now, does it really mean you're broken? Is it really so unacceptable to feel hurt when someone is unkind to you?"

"I don't want to feel this way," said Leah quietly. "I came here to you because I wanted to *fix* myself. Don't you get it?"

"And what would your compassionate observer say to that?"

"Ugh, I don't even want to do that anymore. I hate that whole game!" Leah said, then immediately regretted her words. "Dr. Amanda, I'm sorry. I didn't mean that. I just . . . I just want to run away right now."

"I can see that. You're feeling so bad right now."

"So what am I supposed to do now, huh? What exercise is there for this?"

"Well . . ." said Dr. Amanda, "what if there isn't an exercise? What if we just . . . give you permission to feel as bad as you feel?"

"I don't get it."

"Well, you feel bad, right?"

"Not bad. *Awful*."

"Okay. So, let's just sit with that for a moment."

"But . . . why would I want to sit with it? To feel even worse?"

It took a long while for Leah to calm down and for Dr. Amanda to start getting through to her. Dr. Amanda could remain calm, relatively speaking, because she had seen all this before. There could often be an unconscious expectation that therapy, once "complete," would spare a person from the indignity of having to feel any strong, unpleasant emotions ever again. In popular culture, there was a strong suggestion that therapy was about fixing things permanently.

The implication was that if you were only psychologically healthy enough, then you never had to experience the discomfort of a negative emotion—you would henceforth always be enlightened, invulnerable, perfectly optimistic about everything, confident, strong. All things were easy for you. You just grew and grew forever.

Kind of unrealistic, right?

We might picture the final product of therapy as someone who was immune to all negative feelings, unable to ever be hurt; someone who was never wrong, never jealous or angry or petty; someone who always had the answers to every problem; someone who was never confused or tired or doubtful; someone who was independent and needed nobody and nothing . . .

Leah felt good when she was able to make changes to her worldview and receive a broadly positive response from those around her. Her self-esteem was growing. Unfortunately, that sense of self-esteem was *still dependent on external validation*. Self-esteem could be thought of as rather shallow. It meant that when we achieved and were healthy and happy, then we felt good about who we were. When people liked us and approved of us, then we felt great. The converse was that when we failed or when we didn't feel strong or when people didn't approve of us, that "self-esteem" flew out the window. It was conditional all along.

What Dr. Amanda was trying to point Leah to was something **unconditional**—a true, deep acceptance of who she was independent of external events or other people's opinions. Leah thought that Dr. Amanda wanted her to *like* feeling bad, or to agree with it. She mistakenly thought that accepting one's negative feelings was about doing something to prolong or condone them. But really, Dr. Amanda only wanted her to accept how she felt—to acknowledge that it was her truth right now.

"Tell me something, Leah. You used a word a moment ago—*shouldn't*. You seemed to say that you shouldn't be feeling bad right now."

"No. I should have figured this out. This is my seventh session, and it's stupid to be back at square one again."

"You feel like there is something wrong with how you feel. Like it's some kind of mistake."

"Of course it is. I was supposed to be over all this already."

"Should. Supposed to. You're making a lot of demands on yourself here, Leah, and making a lot of comparisons to . . . who knows who. I want to come back to those comparisons in just a moment. But . . . you *do* feel the way you feel. You do feel bad. That's the truth for you right now."

"But . . . I have to get over this, Dr. Amanda . . . I have to figure all this out or . . ."

"Or what?"

"No one will love me if I don't change who I am."

Leah couldn't believe what she had said. It seemed like an outrageous thing to confess to. She felt as though she was suddenly naked in the room, all her vulnerabilities on display.

"Leah, what if I told you that the problem here is not that others won't accept you . . . but that you're not accepting yourself?"

What followed was a long, difficult conversation about what acceptance actually meant. Following these absolute terms—should, have to, supposed to—Dr. Amanda showed Leah that there were actually two things happening: the way she felt and the way she felt *about* the way she felt. Her primary emotion and her secondary emotion. Leah felt bad. But then she also felt that this reaction was wrong somehow, inferior, stupid. She felt that this badness was proof that she "had relapsed," as she put it, that she hadn't made progress at all, and that deep down, this meant that she was no longer eligible for people's love or care.

Leah wanted to jump in and "fix" her primary emotion, make it go away, and access all those pleasant, easy feelings of mastery she'd discovered in the earlier sessions. Here, Dr.

Amanda might have gone along with Leah's appraisal and quickly rushed in with yet another CBT exercise. Yet she didn't. She knew that it was time to dig a little deeper. Leah's core belief was "if people don't like me, then I'm bad." She had progressed halfway along the path—she was beginning to see that other people did and could respond positively to her. But now came the real challenge—could Leah still retain a sense of dignity, maturity, and self-worth in the face of people just, well, not liking her?

"I keep saying it a million different ways, Leah, but my job as a therapist isn't to help you be better at your dysfunction. It isn't to agree with your core belief and help you construct a world in line with that."

The conversation had become heavy and raw, but there was enough trust now that Leah was able to speak freely, even though things felt uncomfortable . . . painful, even.

"But I still don't get what you're talking about. Your job is to help me feel better."

"Remember that man and the mouse we talked about ages ago?" said Dr. Amanda.

"How could you ever let me forget about *him*?" Leah laughed, bringing a little levity to the situation.

"Well, the thing that would have made him feel really good was to agree with him that his mouse was his secret charm to keeping him safe. In fact, if I had given him *another* mouse, then he would have thought I was a great therapist, that I really cared for him and wanted him to be safe. You see what I'm saying? Your core belief is that unless other people approve of you and validate you, then you're nothing. You're worthless. The only way I can break this belief is to keep showing you that you have worth, that you can accept yourself exactly as you are, whether people approve of you or not. I'm not here to flatter you or tell you lies, Leah. If you told me that people had been unkind to you and that it hurt, and my response was to quickly find a way for you to change so that people liked you again, then what would I be saying? It would be like agreeing with them. I'd be saying, 'Leah, there's something wrong with you for being upset that people don't like you. The way you're doing things is wrong.' *But you are upset.* If I rejected that feeling, I would be rejecting what is real for you right now. I'd be rejecting *you*."

"I just..." Leah sighed deeply. "I get what you're saying. I just can't see the point in dwelling on that feeling."

"Not dwelling. Just allowing. I don't want you to make that feeling bigger. I don't want you to make it smaller. I don't want you to interpret it or judge it or measure it so you can see how it compares to someone else's feelings. I don't want you to rate it at all. I just want you to see it and acknowledge that it's real for you."

"Well. Fine. I acknowledge it. I'll be really honest with you . . ."

"Be as honest as you can!"

"I'm . . . scared. I'm really scared that I'm just going to be like this forever. Just a messed up, useless person. And that I can never change."

Dr. Amanda had her pen out again. She wrote the words on her notepad, tore the page out, and held it up between them.

"This here, Leah," she said, "is how you feel right now. It's a big knot of feelings and thoughts and perceptions. Right now, it's *here*." She held the paper close up to Leah's face, so close there was only an inch or two of space between them.

"What can you see of the room when this feeling is this close to you?" Dr. Amanda asked.

"Uh . . . not much."

"How big is the feeling?"

"How big? It takes up my whole field of vision."

"And how does it feel?"

Leah laughed. "It feels really claustrophobic. All I can do is read the words over and over." She squirmed in her seat to try to avoid the intrusive page.

"Okay, what about now?" Dr. Amanda said as she moved the piece of paper away and slightly to the side.

"I can still see it, but I can see some of the room now."

"Yes, that's right. The feeling's still here, though, right? It hasn't changed?"

Leah looked at the words and read them again in her mind. *I'm scared that I'm going to be like this forever, and that I can never change.* No, that hadn't changed. It still hurt.

"It's still there. It's just . . . not the only thing I'm seeing," said Leah, understanding the exercise.

Dr. Amanda put the paper on an empty chair at the far side of the room.

"I just want to put it there for now, Leah," she said. "I don't need to tear it up or set fire to it or have a big argument with it. At the same time, I don't want to focus on it so much that it's the only thing I can see."

"Because when you argue with it, you're still focusing on it. It still takes up your whole field of vision. I think I understand," said Leah.

"Now," said Dr. Amanda, "let's leave that paper there. Let's have respect for it. And let's carry on our conversation. Emotions are here to be felt. There's nothing wrong with emotions—and we can't deny them even if we try. But we don't have to let them control or distract us. Some of us get stuck in our emotions, even hypnotized by them. Some of us get some relief by tearing up the paper or burning it, pretending it's not there. They feel like they can only be happy and healthy once all those little papers are gone forever. But . . ."

"But they come back. Like this one came back for me," said Leah.

"Right," said Dr. Amanda. "So, if it's going to be there one way or another, let's see what it feels like to just . . . let it be there."

Reflect

- Therapy can get confusing and muddled at times. It can feel risky, emotional, and sometimes very exposing. What Leah and Dr. Amanda are doing here is messy work. The kind of work where it's difficult to pull out one single, easy thematic thread that will make everything make sense. But gradually, Leah is learning new skills and new ways of perceiving things. Dr. Amanda is not letting her off lightly! What do you make of this new turn of events?
- Dr. Amanda has identified that Leah is placing demands on herself about how she should be feeling, how fast she should be improving, how happy she should feel,

and how easy she should be finding the process. Dr. Amanda doesn't reassure her in this regard or try to tell her that everything will be okay (i.e., a load of "positivity"). Instead, she keeps coming back to the *negative* feelings Leah is actually experiencing in the moment. Why?

If most of us are honest, we quietly hope that therapy will be something that makes our lives permanently easier, simpler, and fairer. Pop psychology and conventional self-help tells us stories of people who, once they finally developed enough self-belief, were finally able to get the promotion, get the girl, get the life they really wanted. The truth is, therapy isn't about teaching us to be perfect and immune to life's inevitable trouble—it's to help us become wiser, more mature, and better able to live with, and in, that trouble. In fact, "If I just have enough self-love, then I'll finally live the life I'm meant to be living" is just another way of saying "I only deserve to be happy and fulfilled once I'm perfect." This is not all that different from Leah's damaging core belief that she can only be a good person and happy with herself if others approve of her first.

Imagine a young, nerdy guy with low self-esteem and difficulty with dating. The "positive" solution is one where he grows his confidence, takes the risk, and starts chatting to girls he likes. Because of his confidence, the story goes, he comes across as far more likeable, and women respond differently to him. Therapy taught him to be confident in himself, he overcame his problems, and in the end, he got what he wanted all along—the attention of the women he was interested in.

But is this really a happy ending? What would have happened if the guy in our story built up his confidence, learned to love himself like a pro . . . and then proceeded to get rejected by women at precisely the rate as he always had been rejected? Would that mean his therapy failed? Would it mean that he still needed to work on his confidence?

The uncomfortable truth is that life inevitably brings loss, confusion, awkwardness, boredom, unfairness, pain, insult, obstacle, difficulty . . . Every person has within them a series of flaws and weaknesses, and we are all limited by our biology, our demographics, our history, and sometimes just random chance.

Psychological wellness comes from changing the way we encounter these things—not in how well we succeed in avoiding or denying them.

- Who can you forgive today—not because they "deserve" it or because they have redeemed themselves, but just because? Do you need to forgive yourself?

- What truth needs telling right now? Instead of denying how you really feel, what's it like to just be honest and acknowledge what is real for you?
- Try to let go of global, totalizing, all-or-nothing words like *everything*, *nothing*, *always*, and so on, and get some perspective. You may experience some pretty strong negative emotions. But they are *not* permanent, they do *not* expand to include every aspect of your life, and they do *not* say something absolute about you as a person or the world. Can you look for ways to set your feelings to one side—just like Dr. Amanda set the paper on the chair—not making it smaller or bigger than it is, but just *sitting with* it?

Session 8

It was Christmas time. The days grew short and grey, and the year itself seemed to loosen up, tired after a long year of schedules and to-do lists. Leah canceled a few sessions with Dr. Amanda so she could spend some time back home with her family. Dr. Amanda cleared her schedule and did the same. Still, the two women were on one another's minds. As Leah went about her days, she found herself wondering now and then, *What would Dr. Amanda say right now?* In the same way, Dr. Amanda couldn't help occasionally thinking, *Where is Leah now? And how is she doing?*

Part of Leah felt a little nervous to give up her weekly sessions for a while, secretly wondering if the wheels would come off without Dr. Amanda there. She liked and missed Dr. Amanda.

Were they friends? Not really. But somehow, they were more than friends. More than once, Leah had caught herself thinking that what she really wanted was to show Dr. Amanda how much progress she'd made. She allowed herself to daydream about that moment in the unclear future where she could sit up proudly in her seat and say, "Dr. Amanda, I don't need you anymore." In a nice way, of course.

When Leah arrived for session eight, she was feeling so very different about things than she had a few months before. Dr. Amanda had given her lots to read, lots of worksheets to complete, and one or two (frankly terrifying) "behavioral experiments" to try. In other words, they had a lot to catch up on.

The two chatted happily about the Christmas holidays and all the usual cozy topics of conversation that rose naturally that time of year—playful gripes about overeating, dealing with difficult relatives, how much it had snowed. But the small talk quickly gave way to the juicier topics that both had been eager to tackle again.

"So . . . I did the experiments," Leah said with a grin.

"Amazing. Well done you. Tell me all about it."

"Well . . . it was interesting. I decided to do the banana exercises, remember?"

Here, Leah was referring to what was sometimes called a "shame-attacking" exercise—people who struggled with assertiveness, low self-esteem, and inhibition were challenged to do something wildly out of their comfort zones just to prove to themselves that not only could they do it, and not only did their worst prediction not come true, but in a strange way, they even enjoyed it! Common shame-attacking exercises included asking strangers for money, ordering a pair of shoes for dinner at a restaurant, riding the escalator standing backward, or taking a banana for a walk on a piece of string around the mall—this was why Leah called these activities "banana exercises."

Leah had given herself the task of saying exactly what she'd thought of her aunt's perennially awful Christmas gifts, and also of wearing something outrageously glamorous and over the top to a Christmas party. Though she was pretty sure she would die from embarrassment doing either of these things, she did them.

"So did you die?" asked Dr. Amanda.

Leah laughed. "Well, that's the funny thing. In all of these worst-case scenarios I dream up for myself, I always sort of stop the movie right at the scariest part, you know? It's like I can't even imagine what happens next because I just don't think about it. But actually, the movie keeps going after that, doesn't it? It was really scary, and my heart was going a thousand miles an hour . . . and then . . . I don't know, then life just carried on!"

"So, you said to your aunt, 'This is the worst gift I've ever received,' and then later you also went out to that party, dressed to the nines, dressed like you were going to a ball, and . . . ?"

"It was a bit weird; I'm not going to lie. But in a way it was also freeing."

"Because after you do this thing that your brain is telling you that you absolutely cannot possibly do or else you'll die . . . you're actually still standing. Still yourself. You *don't* die. You're fine. Even if people stare or get offended, life moves on, as you say. It's a great realization when you see that you can easily survive even mortal humiliation!"

"The funny thing is, just those two exercises have made me so much more relaxed. Like, I just don't care as much anymore! I notice myself speaking up more now. I'm not thinking about it; I just speak. It's kind of easier now. And I don't mind if I offend people—I mean, I don't *want* to offend them—but I think, well, it's okay if people get offended now and then. That's life, right?" she said, and shrugged her shoulders.

Dr. Amanda thought the Leah sitting in front of her really was a world away from the Leah she had seen in the first session, who had been slumped in her chair and had chronically apologized.

"You are still you, and you still have value as a human being whether people like you or don't like you."

"Yeah. I guess so. I'm just who I am. You know, Dr. Amanda, I really want to be my best self. I know you always talk about acceptance and sitting with your emotions and all that. And I think I'm getting better at that. I don't know, there's this woman I follow on Instagram. She's really good at this kind of thing. I admire her. She's totally authentic. She's confident . . . but like, not in a fake way."

"You haven't mentioned her before. She's someone you look up to?"

"Let's just say I'd kill for her life. She says a lot of the same stuff you do, by the way. She's really smart and successful. I kind of think I should be doing something like that, you know?"

"There's that word *should* again."

"I know, I know. But like, she's my age and she's written a book already, and she even gives talks and things. *She* suffered shyness and low self-esteem, too, but she overcame it."

"So, she's like you, then?"

"No way . . . she's better!"

One look at Dr. Amanda's wry smile and Leah jumped in again. "I know, you think I'm making comparisons again!"

"Are you?"

"Well, I guess I am."

"Look, Leah, not all comparisons are bad. It's human to compare ourselves to others. But there's a difference between being inspired and encouraged by a comparison, and being demotivated by it because we think that them being great means that we are less than."

Leah sighed.

"I'm trying to cut back on social media. I already know it makes me feel like crap."

"Tell me why it does."

"Well, you already know. I look at all the stuff people are doing with their lives, and I feel so small, so insignificant... even if I felt pretty good about myself to start with. Some people are just so annoyingly successful, you know? They have everything, and you can't help but look at yourself, and your life just looks like garbage in comparison."

"Ouch. Sounds like quite a painful thought. What do you want to do with it?"

"I want to . . . like I said, I want to quit spending so much time on social media. I know I need to do that. But this girl I follow, though, I don't know. Writing a book, giving talks..."

"Do *you* want to write a book?" Dr. Amanda asked.

"Uh... not really?"

Dr. Amanda shrugged. "Then don't write one."

"Yeah, you're right."

"Maybe this woman wanted to write a book, and she did that, and that's great for her. Maybe she didn't really want to write one but just felt like she had to. Either way, what does it help you to compare yourself to her? She's a different person. Different values. Different goals."

"I know. I guess I'm jealous or something. She has like billions and billions of fans. It's crazy. She posts a single pic of herself and her Christmas tree and her dog, and she gets mountains of compliments."

"Do *you* want to post a picture of your life to billions of people?"

"Hmm..." Leah said, and chewed her lip. "I guess that's just me looking for external validation again, huh?"

Dr. Amanda smiled. "It's normal to look around you in the world and try to see how you measure up, try to understand who you are and what value you hold, what your place is. Other people can give us valuable feedback, and they can support and encourage us. But that is not the *source* of our worth as human beings. You've seen that. I love social media because it makes the search for external validation very obvious—we have all taught ourselves that the number of likes and compliments is directly connected to how valuable we are."

"But if you tie your self-worth to what other people say, then you're always going to be at their mercy. Then it's conditional, like you said."

"Do you think this woman on Instagram is a worthwhile, valuable human being?"

"Of course."

"Do you think she deserves understanding, kindness, and acceptance for who she is as a person?"

"Sure."

"If she lost all her followers overnight and disappeared off social media, and you never heard from her again, would any of that change?"

"She'd . . . she'd still be who she was."

"You're who you are—and you're entitled to the same respect, kindness, and understanding as she is—and it has nothing to do with what social media says or what random strangers say or don't say."

"Yeah, you're right."

"What do you think it would look like for us to appraise how far *you've* come, but without comparing it to other people?"

Leah was stumped.

"Well, I'll give you a hint—do you remember what our first session was like?"

Leah broke into a broad smile. "Oh, I see what you mean! Maybe we can compare where I am now to where I was then, instead of comparing me to the people on Instagram."

"You got it."

"Dr. Amanda, I *have* come a long way. A few months ago I couldn't even think about talking up in class, and now I'm doing it all the time. I really have been making changes, and I've worked hard..."

"It sounds to me like you've got a taste of internal validation."

Leah thought about this for a moment.

"If you didn't feel that way about yourself, if you didn't feel proud about the progress you've made and the hard work you've put in, then do you think any number of Instagram followers would change that for you?"

It was like a lightbulb had gone off in Leah's mind.

"You're right, Dr. Amanda. It wouldn't make a difference."

"Look, Leah, we're all human. We all like a bit of praise and recognition. We want to feel like we have a place in the world and that we have a valued contribution. So, I want to say it now: *I'm* proud of you and how far you've come. I recognize the progress you've made, and I want to tell you it's great. But I also want you to build the kind of self-worth where you'd be able to be proud of you *even if I wasn't.* Do you understand?"

Leah nodded. "But . . . that doesn't mean I have to be a complete narcissist about everything, either. I can be comfortable in who I am, both good and bad qualities. I'm a human being. I have the same right as anyone else to be here," Leah said, as though she were continuing Dr. Amanda's trail of thought and making it her own. Leah felt like she was on the brink of something big, something she couldn't quite see yet, but she was just beginning to feel.

It was something so different to everything that came before it. A new idea emerged in her mind: that maybe she could accept and love herself right now, *as she was*. Not at some distant point in the future when she would somehow feel braver and more together than she did now. Not later, once she tidied up the last few of these lingering problems. But now. *Right now*. Sure, she would still carry on working on her blind spots and do her best; she would still work hard and be honest and try her best in everything. But in the meantime, why not just . . . relax? Why not just accept who she was? That was *Leah*—nobody else.

"I wanted to give you something," said Dr. Amanda as she rummaged in one of her drawers. She produced an old, laminated A4 sheet that looked like it had been around a few years. She handed it to Leah.

PERSONAL BILL OF RIGHTS

1. *I have the right to ask for what I want.*
2. *I have the right to say no.*
3. *I have the right to express all my feelings—positive and negative.*
4. *I have the right to change my mind.*
5. *I have the right to make mistakes and to not be perfect.*
6. *I have the right to my own values and beliefs.*
7. *I have the right to determine my own priorities.*
8. *I have the right to be myself.*
9. *I have the right to say, "I don't know."*
10. *I have the right to be treated with dignity and respect.*

"What do you think of that? I especially like number five."

Leah read the page and nodded. "You like number five? The right to be imperfect?"

"It's often one of the last gifts we want to give ourselves, I find."

Reflect

- Acceptance and self-worth go hand in hand. If we cannot accept ourselves, we may end up playing out all the same old core beliefs that keep us trapped in seeking external validation—and then feeling bad when life is inevitably difficult, unkind, or negative. Why do you think Dr. Amanda chose number five—the right to be imperfect—as her favorite on the list of "personal bill of rights"? What does giving ourselves this right actually look like?
- Leah tended to use comparison to others as an external way to measure her self-worth, i.e., she didn't look like the people she admired on social media. But external validation can come from many different avenues. Where do you most seek validation? Do you have your own sense of personal validation that comes from within?
- Dr. Amanda bluntly asks Leah if she actually wants to write a book or be a social media personality herself. Why do you think she does this? Perhaps she

could have gone further and asked exactly what Leah *did* want to do, if not that. This might have been the first step in identifying and orienting toward her own values, rather than looking externally to find those values in other peoples' lives.

Leah has come a long way since the first session. She's taken great leaps toward uncovering her core negative belief and has become better at recognizing smaller thoughts and perceptions that stem from this. She's directly challenged these thoughts and beliefs by taking *action* and doing experiments, then being brave enough to update her perceptions based on the feedback she receives. She's slowly beginning to realize that she is a person with value and worth who deserves care and respect (from herself most importantly!) and that she doesn't have to win other people's approval or be perfect first.

To start condensing all of Leah's lessons down, take a look at the following steps for processing your own emotions in the same way:

Step 1: Acknowledge and accept the emotion you have without judgment, interpretation, clinging, or avoidance. Give your feelings a name and a label. Slow down and pay attention to what you're thinking, and get some distance between you and the temporary experience. Remind yourself that these experiences are *not permanent, pervasive, or personal.* The feeling will pass; it doesn't spread to include the entire universe, and it doesn't say something eternal about you as a person.

Step 2: Validate yourself and give yourself permission to feel what you feel without rushing in to fix yourself or escape the experience. Try saying things like, "It's okay to feel this way," or, "Anxiety is uncomfortable, but it's not dangerous," or, "I have the right to feel as I do."

Step 3: From a place of compassion and understanding, reflect on what's happening and what you want to do next. What are your values? What are your goals? Use these to guide your next action, rather than be guided by needing to escape or avoid.

Step 4: Gently turn your attention to some thought and perception that feels more helpful, kinder, or more realistic to you. Try to remove all-or-nothing phrasing and replace it with something more nuanced and which respects your humanity.

For example:

Step 1: "I'm feeling ashamed and embarrassed now. I'm thinking that old thought I always think—that I'm worthless. But I'm trying to remember that even though I feel like that now, I haven't always felt that way and won't feel this way forever. There are lots of areas of my life where I feel comfortable and confident. This feeling is unpleasant, but it doesn't define me."

Step 2: "It's okay to feel ashamed sometimes, especially if someone deliberately makes fun of you! I'm only human. Most people would feel as I do right now. It's normal to feel bad sometimes."

Step 3: "Okay, so some people were very critical and judgmental of me today. That's something *they* did. But what do I want to do now? I like who I am, and I value my uniqueness. So I'm going to focus on what matters to me. I refuse to let this stop me from expressing myself or contributing or engaging with life."

Step 4: "I refuse to think this thought, *I'm worthless*. I'm going to choose instead to tell myself that I am a worthwhile person with good and bad qualities. I can say I *feel* worthless rather than I *am* worthless. That feels more reasonable and useful to me."

Session 9

A curious thing can start to happen to people as they develop more robust psychological health, grow more resilient, and begin to challenge old, limiting patterns of self-belief. Dr. Amanda is familiar with how paradoxical some of these things can seem: On the one hand, her clients grow in leaps in bounds; on the other, they start encountering *new* problems. Why?

Imagine a person with agoraphobia (a fear of leaving the house and of crowds) who works hard to overcome that fear. They genuinely find ways to get on top of the intense fear they have every time they walk out the door. But something else happens: They are suddenly confronted with the normal, everyday problem of the stress and hassle of interacting with other people as they go about their day. This new challenge is unexpected and sometimes demoralizing—the person with agoraphobia is so busy overcoming the big fear that they never realize their lack of skill in managing the small, everyday fears—the ones that everyone deals with as a matter of course. The ones they were able to avoid, essentially, by staying indoors.

Consider another example. Someone who has worked hard to reverse a pathological shyness and timidity (well, yes, let's say the "someone" is Leah) may discover with a jolt that there is a whole world out there—a world they never had to interact with before under the cover of their old negative patterns. Leah made immense progress when she started to challenge her black-and-white thinking about other people (they *all* dislike me, they're *all* the same, and I'm the only one who's different . . .). She discovered that there was a whole universe of grey area she had never really appreciated before. And she would need to learn to navigate that grey area.

For Leah, the big lesson is to learn that she is not, in fact, worthless. She has value and dignity as a human being. She can love and accept herself and is someone who has as much right to take up space in the world as anyone else. And that is a mammoth mountain to climb! Now that she's climbed that mountain, however, she finds herself in the more ordinary, "normal" realm and realizes that every day there are dozens of smaller hills and valleys she has to traverse.

There are conversations that can only be navigated with sophisticated communication skills; there are minor conflicts and misunderstandings to resolve; there are annoyances and small obligations that can't be avoided; there are times of boredom. Leah has a new set of ideas: Some people will like her; some won't. Now, her work is living in that complex, varied space—which paradoxically is a lot harder than the space she occupied when she could issue a blanket statement about all humanity and not think about it again.

The person overcoming depression is not just learning to let go of deep and unhealthy despair—they are also learning how to experience ordinary, rational sadness.

The person overcoming anxiety is not just learning to question the assumption that everything always leads to their most catastrophic feared outcomes—they are also learning how to experience ordinary, rational nervousness and aversion to things they ought to be worried about.

The person overcoming a deep sense of self-loathing and shame about themselves is learning unconditional acceptance—but they also have to learn that occasionally, they are perfectly capable of being the bad guy, and they can act in ways that should cause a little regret or remorse.

All of this is easy to observe from afar, but more difficult to understand in your own life. Mature, well-developed people are capable of nuance. They can be patient with themselves and others, they can accept situations even when they're muddy and unresolved, and they can allow themselves to inhabit a world that is complex, flawed, and changing. Similarly, they allow *themselves* and other people to be complex, flawed, and changing. As session nine approaches, Leah is wondering how it can be that the more she grows and the more she understands about herself, the more work there needs to be done. She doesn't know how to express any of this to Dr. Amanda.

"I've been reading a lot, Dr. Amanda," she said. Leah was really enjoying the sense of closeness and trust between the two now, even as she sensed that their time together wouldn't last very much longer.

"That sounds good. You're really taking responsibility for things."

"Exactly. Responsibility—that's exactly it. I think I realize now why I was having so much trouble when I first came to see you."

"Yeah? Tell me."

"Well, I was telling a story. A story about myself. But in this story I was always a loser, always going to be a loser. I told a story I couldn't get out of!"

"But you can see that story now."

"Yes, I think so. That's the crazy thing—I used my own free will to make up a story about myself where I didn't really have free will. Does that make sense?"

"I think that makes a lot of sense," Dr. Amanda said. This was the point in therapy that she liked best. The point where, wobbling only slightly, the client whizzed ahead on their own, the training wheels no longer necessary. She especially liked the nervous, slightly excited attitude that always happened at this point—it was like the client turning back to check that the therapist was still there. They seemed to say, *Look, I'm doing it! I am doing it, right?*

"I think I'm really starting to get that... how this story is not something that other people are doing to me. It's something I'm doing to myself. That's why you made me do all those stupid things, the banana exercises, you know?"

"Why?"

"Because you wanted me to see... to see that it was *me* who was doing it."

Outside, the sun had already gone down. It was the depths of winter. The two looked out the window. Things were waiting underground,

Leah thought, waiting for spring to come so they could grow.

"You seem troubled," said Dr. Amanda.

Leah sighed. "I don't know. I feel . . . kind of scared. But scared in a different way than I ever have been before. It's like . . . I'll tell you what it's like. Imagine you had been a prisoner all your life, and then one day you were free. The prison vanished, poof! And there you were, standing in the middle of nowhere. Completely free . . ."

"How does that feel?"

Leah laughed. "Kind of terrifying! I don't know. All my life I've told myself that I'm worthless, that I'm the shy one, the weirdo. It's going to sound strange, but it took all the courage in the world to start to imagine that I didn't *have to* be that person anymore. That I could be somebody else. And I'm happy that I understand that now. It's just . . ."

"What now?" Dr. Amanda ventured.

"Exactly. That's exactly what I'm thinking. *What now?* For the first time in my life, I'm really excited about things, and there's so much I want to do. But it's all overwhelming. I want to do the best I can, be the best I can . . ."

"You've done a fantastic thing. You've replaced your need for external validation with your own inner sense of value and worth. You're asking yourself questions you haven't asked before—like, *Who am I really? What do I truly want to do with my life? What is my soul really yearning for?* Those are big questions."

"And they're *scary* questions! Now suddenly everything is up in the air. Do I really want to continue with this degree at all? Why did I start with it? I can't honestly say. Should I take a break and think things over? Then there are things with my dad, all this drama with my aunt, my ex . . . How should I approach any of that? What would be the best thing to do? I'm reading so much now, you know, and learning so much, but it's all overwhelming . . ."

"Leah, woah, slow down. Tell me what's happening right now."

This was something Dr. Amanda had started introducing into sessions. She called it "grounding." She'd pause now and again to reconnect the conversation to the present moment. It was a little window of awareness that allowed them both to take a breather and remember where they were. And inevitably, where they always found themselves was *here* and *now*.

Leah exhaled loudly and relaxed. "Phew! What's happening . . . I'm . . . There's a lot of anxiety right now."

"Okay, good. You've put a label on it. Tell me where it is in your body."

Leah knew the drill. She raised her hand to her throat. "It's here. I feel a tightness here and all down my neck."

"Okay. Good. Let's just stop for a moment. There are quite a lot of thoughts buzzing around in your head right now."

"Yeah, tons of them. They're all quite . . . stressful. They're all kind of rushing and urgent, like each one of them is demanding I look at it or else."

"Okay. That's good. Let's take a breath . . ." Dr. Amanda demonstrated, "and let's figure out what we want to choose right now. If you follow those thoughts, where do they go?"

Leah thought for a moment. "They lead to me feeling powerless. And afraid."

Dr. Amanda said nothing. She could have said, *Do you want to feel that way?* but at this point, she was trying to teach Leah to do that for herself. She waited.

"They lead me to this weird place . . . where I'm not in control. You know, Dr. Amanda, they lead me straight back to that prison. The one I was telling you about where I'm just a victim and a loser and a black sheep. That's where it goes."

"One choice is to grab hold of those anxious thoughts and let them take you wherever they want."

"I don't want to do that. I want to try something else," said Leah.

She rubbed her head. This was so hard.

"Gah, I don't know!" she said at last. "Dr. Amanda, what's wrong with me? Do you think this is all just an elaborate defense mechanism so I don't have to face my fears? Is this *resistance*? I've been reading all about it. Maybe my unconscious mind is trying to get in my way and sabotage all the good work I've done. But on the other hand, how do you know? Maybe my unconscious mind is actually my intuition, my gut feeling trying to keep me safe. I think this is all my mother again, and the major complexes she gave me. It's like an intergenerational thing—I've been reading about that, too, by the way—I sometimes wonder if, like, her trauma came down to me in my genetics or something. If I'm almost doomed to play out her psychological demons, you know? Is that crazy? Is the fact that I'm even asking those questions a red flag? I know I'm not supposed to be checking in with you to get your recognition and all that, but what do you think? What do you *really* think?"

Dr. Amanda gave a wry smile. "Hmm . . . I think you're really letting those anxious thoughts have their way with you."

Leah couldn't help bursting into laughter.

"You're overthinking it," said Dr. Amanda plainly.

"But I'm not really . . . I'm doing what you taught me . . . I'm challenging myself, and I'm solving problems."

"Overthinking can feel like problem-solving. But I'll tell you how you can tell the difference. Problem-solving eventually stops. It leads to one of two things—action or acceptance. Is your line of thought right now leading you to either of those things?"

Leah thought long and hard but had to eventually shake her head.

"Overthinking goes round and round, whereas real problem-solving is focused and linear. It goes somewhere. Overthinking can give us the illusion that we are in control, that we are doing something . . . all the while keeping us trapped and ineffectual. You say you've been doing a lot of reading?"

"Yeah, you know . . . just self-help books and stuff."

"What effect do you think all this reading is having on you?"

"What effect? Well, I think it mostly helps. But . . . you're right in that it's not exactly making me *do* anything."

"Leah, don't get me wrong, reading up about stuff like this, trying to educate yourself, that's a really good impulse."

"I'm just trying to understand more about myself, you know?"

"That sounds great. More understanding. More information . . ."

"Yes, that's all . . ." She studied Dr. Amanda's face. "You don't think it's a good idea, do you?"

Dr. Amanda shrugged. "It's not about what I think, Leah. You should do what's right for you, whether I approve or not. But I am curious about whether it *is* right for you."

"Dr. Amanda?"

"Yes?"

"This is our ninth session, and some time back we sort of suggested that we would do ten sessions together."

"That's right."

"Can you just . . . can you just tell me what you really think? One person to another?"

Dr. Amanda took a deep breath. "Leah, what exactly are you asking me? Would you like me to give you some kind of diagnosis? Tell you my personal opinion? Even if I did, what would happen next? You asked me to speak to you one person to another. Okay, I will. Here's what I think. I think you're at a delicate juncture in your life, at a kind of vulnerable place in the therapy process. Like you say, we'll soon part ways. That means you have to start doing a lot of this stuff on your own. Because you're smart, you've already started to take steps. You're reading self-help, you're thinking deeply about things. Well, no, let me say that differently—you're ruminating about things."

"Am I ruminating? Or am I just . . . increasing my psychological literacy. My awareness?"

"And what do you plan to *do* with all this awareness?"

The question caught Leah off guard.

"You asked me to tell you what I really think. I'll tell you that sometimes people can overthink as a way to avoid actually *doing* things in their lives. They can ruminate so they feel like they're doing something even while they do nothing."

"You think that's what I'm doing?"

"I think it's a question worth asking."

Leah looked deflated. But Dr. Amanda did have this annoying talent for spying the fatal flaw in things and helpfully pointing it out. "Old Leah" would have been mortally offended at this kind of observation. New Leah, however, was reluctantly curious.

"I have been feeling pretty tense lately," she said at last. "Now that I think of it, it is kind of scary, knowing that we'll be finished with sessions soon. I don't want you to misunderstand me; things are going really well. I'm well. It's just . . . there's suddenly so much to worry about."

"I get that, Leah. Change can be really hard. Even if that change is an improvement."

Leah nodded.

"I am getting overwhelmed. There's so much I want to do, so many changes I want to make, so many things going on in my life . . ."

"And you're perfectly able to manage each and every one of them," Dr. Amanda said, "but you'll have to tackle them one at a time."

For the next ten minutes, Dr. Amanda gave Leah an unexpected homework project: She instructed her to *deliberately* worry. She told Leah that every day, she was to set aside some time expressly to worry, and nothing else. Leah was to schedule this fixed period "worry time" and, when the time came, worry as hard as she could. The rule, however, was that she couldn't worry outside of that time. When an anxious thought popped into her mind, she was to notice it there and tell it, "Hello, worry. I see you. I'm going to give you all the attention you want from me . . . but not now. We'll worry when I say so." Then she was to note the worry down in a book and do whatever she could to forget about it until her worry time arrived.

In fact, Dr. Amanda handed Leah a small notebook there and then, in the office, and they agreed together on when the daily worry time should commence and how long it should last.

"But . . . what if it doesn't work and I just end up filling page after page of worries? What if I have a whole book's worth of worries by tomorrow afternoon?"

"Aha!" shouted Dr. Amanda, "now *that* sounds like a useless worry if ever I heard one. Let's put that in the book. And then let's forget about it."

Reflect

- As a CBT therapist, much of Dr. Amanda's approach is about increasing her clients' sense of personal responsibility, helping them develop their skills for living, and fostering awareness of ingrained thought patterns that are no longer working. What do you think is the rationale behind the "scheduled worry" exercise? How do you anticipate it playing out in Leah's life?

- Leah touches on an important point—how do we ever know the difference between useful thinking and rumination? When are we dwelling uselessly on an idea, and when are we cultivating awareness? Dr. Amanda shares what she thinks the answer is, but what do you think? What could be a warning sign that you've crossed over from "problem-solving mode" into "rumination mode"?
- Leah starts to overthink just at the point she is starting to make real progress . . . and also at the point where she will soon terminate her relationship with Dr. Amanda. Do you think there's any truth in the idea that overthinking can actually function as a form of avoidance? Leah may read self-help books not to help her live better, but *instead* of living better. Is there anything in your own life that you do to avoid doing the truly difficult and scary stuff?

One technique that Dr. Amanda might have also suggested is the "brain dump." Rather than valiantly trying to force yourself not to ruminate, you can consciously choose to let it all out in a structured way. For example, you could give yourself ten or twenty minutes in the morning to just sit down and write, without censoring yourself and without trying to stop to interpret or organize your thoughts. The idea is that this lets off some of the pressure and paves the way for the next step: decluttering, prioritizing, and organizing your thoughts.

Once everything is written down, go back through it and ask yourself:

- What am I worried about?
- Can I change it? What is my zone of control?
- If I can't change it, what can I do to accept it or at least move on?
- Do I notice any recurring patterns?
- Am I forgetting to pay attention to positive aspects of the situation, things to be grateful for, and important values?
- What do I want to consciously pull my attention away from today?
- Where would be the most important place for me to place my attention instead?

Session 10

"Tell me about this thing you mentioned in your message the other day—the exchange program."

"I can't believe it, but I signed up to express my interest. If I'm interviewed and accepted, they'll send me to China to go and talk about our work at the department and meet some fellow international students," said Leah.

"Wow, that sounds so exciting."

"It is! It'll be two whole weeks we're gone. You've got to understand . . . I've never even left the state. Can you imagine, *me*? Going all the way to China, and when I'm there, giving talks and presentations and meeting all sorts of people . . ."

"What an opportunity! When do you find out whether they've accepted your application or not?"

Here, Leah looked uncomfortable.

"End of next week sometime. But . . . I don't know. I'm not sure if I should have signed up at all. It seemed like a good idea at the time, but now I'm wondering whether I've bitten off more than I can chew."

"Well . . . you certainly don't have to go. You have a little time yet to decide what you want to do."

"I know . . . I don't want to regret anything, of course. It will be ages before they host something like this ever again, if they do. So, if I want to, I have to take my chance now."

"Sounds like it's something you're curious about."

"Sure, but on the *other* hand . . ."

Leah had a bad case of analysis paralysis. She had been doing the "scheduled worry" technique like Dr. Amanda had suggested; she had curbed her voracious self-help book hunger and had been consciously trying to let go when she noticed her mind going round and round in circles. But her mind kept getting jammed on one worry: Did she really have it in her to do this big trip? Yes, she thought so. But was she ready? Really ready? Doing the exchange program was a chance in a lifetime that she'd regret not taking ... but might she also regret taking it, too? The decision was driving her crazy. She felt frozen with uncertainty.

"Leah, I feel like in the beginning of our work together, we focused a lot on your core beliefs, and I'm proud of just how much progress you've made in that area in a relatively short time. Now, this is our final session. Of course, my door is always open, but from here on out, we'll be parting ways."

"I know. It's kind of ... nerve-wracking."

"Well, Leah, a lot of people find the end of therapy a little uncomfortable. It can bring up some feelings, and it can be kind of awkward. But the thing to keep focusing on is that even though what we did in our sessions together is over, in a way, you're just getting started. You're going to go out in the world and go on living, go on making your life what you want it to be, using everything we learned in this room."

Leah sighed.

"What would you say if I told you that feeling a little indecisive right now is perfectly normal?" Dr. Amanda continued.

"It is?"

"Oh, absolutely. You've learned many new skills, but you haven't had all that long to practice them yet. You're a little uncertain of yourself. That's okay."

"I just... don't want to do the wrong thing," Leah said eventually.

Dr. Amanda laughed. "Oh, but you will do the wrong thing sooner or later!" she said. "The thing is, I hope you're a little more aware now that making mistakes doesn't define you, and that whatever happens outside there in the world, *you can handle it*. You have that power."

Leah nodded.

"What do you say to going over a few relaxation exercises today, things you can return to when you're trying to manage these kinds of worries and fears when they crop up?" said Dr. Amanda.

"Sure, okay. You're not going to make me do meditation, are you?"

"No, don't worry, I remember how much you don't like meditation. I want to teach you something a lot simpler and straightforward. It's called four-seven-eight breathing. Have you heard of it?"

"Don't think so."

"Well, it's easy. I want you to try to do this once a day, maybe in the evenings just before you go to bed. Find somewhere you won't be distracted, get comfortable, close your eyes, then just start breathing. You inhale for a count of four, you hold the breath for a count of seven, and then you exhale for a count of eight. So, you just remember four-seven-eight."

"That's it?"

"That's it. All you're doing is focusing on these breaths and counting, and that's all. If your mind starts chattering away again, that's fine. Just focus again on the breathing and on the counting. It's great when you get a good rhythm going. It can be quite hypnotic."

"Sounds like meditation to me!"

"All right, you got me . . . it's a *bit* like meditation. But more like mindfulness. Just focusing on one thing and keeping your attention there. You'd be amazed at how relaxing it is. You focus on the sensations around you, on everything. Sounds, smells, the touch of things."

"And then what?"

"Well, instead of me telling you . . . do you want to just try it right now?"

This was what Leah really loved about working with Dr. Amanda. She never passed up an opportunity to *do* something. She was always encouraging an open, curious mind. She was always brewing up some experiment or other. For the next ten minutes, the two sat together, with Dr. Amanda leading the way with some simple guiding instructions. But soon her voice faded away and both got lost in their own quiet world of breath and sensation.

The first minute or so, Leah's mind was going a thousand miles an hour, and she thought of everything, from how much she hated meditation, to the way Dr. Amanda pronounced her Ts, to the nagging worry that she was doing the exercise wrong. But as they continued to sit, and Leah's breath rose and fell, 4-7-8, and again 4-7-8, she discovered the rhythm Dr. Amanda was talking about. Her mind quietened down a little. She noticed little things in the room she hadn't noticed before. She felt the tension in her neck and shoulders release. When Dr. Amanda spoke again, Leah wasn't sure if one minute had passed or if it had been twenty.

"How did that feel?" she said.

Leah stretched and yawned. It felt . . . good.

"Tell me what happened to all your racing thoughts as you just focused on that breath."

"Well . . . they were there. They were always kind of there. But now and then I forgot about them. I really did just focus on the breath. It was kind of soothing."

"Great. Do you think you can practice that exercise once a day, just for five minutes like that?"

"Woah, was that only five minutes? It felt longer somehow."

"Isn't it funny how stress and tension can mess with our perception of time? What you might like to do is practice just a few breaths in the same way all throughout the day, just whenever you remember. A breath here, a breath there, just when you think of it. All we're trying to do is calm that stress and remind you that all that traffic in your head is just passing noise—you can turn it off anytime."

"I feel like I could have a nap now, honestly."

They both laughed.

"Before you disappear on me, I have one more thing I want to show you."

"Okay."

"Now, don't get mad, but it's also a little like meditation, and it's also got a number name. It's called the five-four-three-two-one method."

"Oh, I think I've actually heard of this one."

"You have? Great! Then you can tell me how it's done."

"Um . . . well, it's this thing where you try to find five things you can see, four things you can hear . . . right? To ground you?"

"That's exactly it. Five things you can see, four things you can hear, three things you can touch, two things you can smell, and one thing you can taste. You just pause, take a few deep breaths, and focus on what's going on around you. I like to think of it as a kind of fuse for overthinking—the best way to get out of a busy head that's full of runaway thoughts is to ground yourself in the concrete world around you. That means your five senses."

"Okay. I get that. Actually, when we did the breathing exercise a moment ago, I noticed that I was suddenly hearing and feeling things I hadn't noticed before."

"Yeah, isn't that interesting how that happens? And I'm sure as you were noticing those sensations, there's one thing you *weren't* doing, right?"

"Yeah, I wasn't thinking about stuff."

"Exactly. You were just present. That's a great cure for stress and anxiety."

"Dr. Amanda, can we try it right now?"

Dr. Amanda agreed, and they both experimented with the grounding exercise. It didn't take long. Leah was impressed with how quickly she could become absorbed in the flutters and sounds outside Dr. Amanda's office, the texture of the seat cushion beneath her, the faint smell on the air that by now she recognized but could never identify beyond "it smells like Dr. Amanda's office." Leah felt like she had learned a new magic trick. And she noticed that even when an intrusive thought burst into her awareness, she needed only to reconnect to the world of her senses again, and it flew away.

"It's like . . . you can't inhabit your senses and think at the same time," Leah said when they had both ended the exercise. Dr. Amanda agreed.

"Anxious ruminations tend to happen in the imagined past or the imagined future, but it's far harder to be anxious when you're simply here, in the present, noticing what is. Even if you happen to be in a stressful situation, it's usually never as bad as what your fearful imagination can conjure up."

"Do you think I could use this when I'm in China, when I'm, like, giving a presentation or meeting someone in their department?"

Dr. Amanda had to suppress a smile.

"*When* you're in China?"

Leah had to smile too. "Yeah, I guess I have made a decision. I mean, I'm terrified. But I was terrified before, when you encouraged me to speak up in class, remember? And now I speak up in class all the time, and I barely even notice it anymore. It's just automatic now. So, while we were doing that grounding exercise, I got to thinking that if I do go to China and take part in the exchange program, then maybe in a few months I'll be looking back on *that* and I'll be able to think of it in the same way—as though it were just ordinary, just like a habit. And having that thought kind of settled things for me. I have to go because I want to be that person."

"Tell me about that person."

"Hmmm . . . that person is . . . she's very calm and confident in herself. She gets nervous at times—often, in fact. But she's really good at doing what she needs to do even though she is nervous."

"Is this girl you're describing an *introvert*, do you think?"

Leah couldn't help laughing again. It had been a while since she had heard that word.

"No . . . no, she's not an introvert. She's intelligent, though, and she likes to think about things deeply. But actually, I think she does enjoy people, and she's curious, you know? She loves learning all sorts of new things, and that's why she pushes herself sometimes—because she knows it will lead somewhere great."

"She sounds like a wonderful person. I'm glad I've had the chance to get to know her," said Dr. Amanda.

Leah blushed furiously. "Dr. Amanda, we only have ten minutes left."

"So we do."

"I just wanted to say thank you."

"You are most welcome. Thank you, too, Leah, for showing up every session, and for letting me be a part of your life these last few months."

"Do you think there's a chance I'll go out there and just mess everything up, and that I'll be back here in your office in a few months, crying my eyes out, and everything will be back to square one?"

Dr. Amanda took her time thinking of a response. "Leah, I don't know what will happen. I'd be lying if I pretended that I do. Some things are probably going to be difficult, yes, I'm sure. On the other hand, you've got the choice of how you'll respond to it. The choice of the kind of stories you'll tell yourself. You have a lot of new tools to manage whatever comes your way. You're strong. And if you do come back in a few months, well, then you come back. Is that the end of the world?"

"No, I guess not."

"I tell all my clients when we reach the end that they can get in touch with me any time. What do you say to scheduling a kind of follow-up session, say, six months from now?"

"Six months? I'll be back from China then . . . okay."

"Then it's settled. Good luck, Leah."

"Thanks, Dr. Amanda."

Reflect

- In the final session, Dr. Amanda spends lots of time teaching Leah a grounding technique and a way to use her breathing to quickly access a state of calm detachment. Why do you think she does this rather than engage with Leah's anxious ruminations over whether she is or isn't ready to consider the China trip?
- Leah came to the very first session with a kind of self-diagnosis—she called herself an "introvert," and much in her life was shaped around and interpreted according to that label. Dr. Amanda never denied that label, nor did she confirm it. How has this allowed Leah to come to her own expanded definition of herself? Many of us are quick to apply certain psychological labels to ourselves in an attempt to explain and justify our behavior. But would Leah have made the progress she did if Dr. Amanda only agreed to work with her inside the limits of this fixed identity she held for herself?
- Leah's narrative about herself is changing. What do you think it is that's allowed her to genuinely entertain alternative ideas about who she is as a person?

Some therapists say that the course of therapy is a little like a plane journey—the takeoff and landing are the most important parts! Leah has a bumpy start, but her ending with Dr. Amanda is very different. Dr. Amanda expresses appreciation and genuine liking for the new persona that Leah is developing, and this moment is a hint of a possible new way for things to develop in the future: a future where Leah can desire and enjoy other people's praise and recognition, but without being dependent on it and without feeling the anxiety of having her entire sense of self hanging on their approval.

As people become more and more "emotionally literate," and as they gain a more sophisticated and nuanced understanding of their own psychology, there is a tendency to get lost in endless self-absorption. Dr. Amanda predicts that this may become an issue for Leah, who is intelligent and dedicated to endless research and "reading up," but who may tend to use this continual data-gathering in an avoidant way. Overthinkers and ruminators tend to suffer from "mental health hypochondria," where every little mental twinge or emotional ripple sends them into an analytical panic. This is understandable—if you have experienced how well therapy can work, you may be tempted to turn to it again and again, almost like an addict returning to their substance.

As we near the end of our book and leave Leah to the responsibility of her own life, without Dr. Amanda's guidance, it's a good time to consider yourself and your own path. Labels can help us talk more intelligently about our distress; psychological theories can help us comprehend why we are where we are today; models of the way the brain works and what it means for the heart and soul can be extremely useful if we want to gain a deeper understanding of who we are and what we want to be. At some point, however, it's worth remembering that the therapy room is an artificial space. It is a place to reflect on reality, but it is not reality. Eventually, we have to walk outside the four walls of the therapy office and engage in real time with our real life as the real people we are.

Leah has worked hard with Dr. Amanda, but in a way her work is only just beginning. She'll head off to China on her university's exchange program and attempt to apply everything she's learned about herself in the only place it matters: "out there." No amount of insight or self-understanding can substitute for lively, dynamic engagement with other (flawed) human beings. No matter the diagnoses we accrue, the explanations we arrive at, or the labels we apply to ourselves, none of it will make the world less complex, less dynamic, and less challenging.

The end goal of therapy, then, is not to make ourselves perfect or perfectly immune from all the damage inherent in being alive. It's not to make us triumphant winners, glossing over the difficult parts of life as though we have a cheat code and want to rush straight to the finish line, where we will be happy and whole and lovable once and for all. Rather, therapy is about helping you become better at living—and that means living all the parts of life, the good and the bad. It means becoming the person you really are and letting that radiate out into the world through conscious action.

Many people are excellent armchair psychologists. They've read all the books and articles, watched all the YouTube videos, and engaged with all the pop-psych out there. Until they take action, however, all of this amounts to nothing except distraction or entertainment. A psychologically healthy person is not someone who is good at going to therapy—it's someone who is good at living life as it is.

The Follow-Up Session

Seven months after Dr. Amanda and Leah's tenth session, Leah returned to complete her "checkup"—and, if she was honest, to brag a little to Dr. Amanda about how well she'd done. She had important news she was bursting to share: She'd met someone, and it was going really well.

"That's great news, Leah!"

"It really is. We've only been seeing each other for a few months now, but I don't know, I have a really good feeling about all of it."

"And the China trip? Come on, you know I'm dying to hear about that!"

"The China trip . . . which one?" Leah laughed, and then she explained. The trip had gone so well that she had been invited back two months later and was now working on a research project with a team there—an accolade she had never dreamed could be hers.

"I did have a few bad weeks, though, I have to admit. Around the anniversary of my mom's death. I know we never really talked about all that, and I think to be honest I wasn't really ready to go there. But all of a sudden it was like a bunch of old memories came flooding back and I was a kid again. You know, Dr. Amanda, I feel like there's a lot of unresolved childhood trauma there."

"What do you mean by that . . . what's childhood trauma?"

By now, Leah was used to Dr. Amanda's Socratic questioning style—the way she always "played dumb" and asked her to explain herself. To Leah it had seemed slightly annoying at first—but she quickly learned that forcing yourself to slow down and explain exactly what you meant usually revealed just how many unfounded assumptions you were working from. In fact, this little habit of questioning her most knee-jerk explanations, interpretations, and assumptions was something she'd picked up from Dr. Amanda, and now she did it herself.

"What do I mean by childhood trauma? Hmm . . . I don't know. Leftover pain from the past? Unresolved things from your childhood that you haven't processed yet?" she ventured.

"Hmm, I see. And what might all this unresolved and unprocessed . . . stuff . . . look like right now, in the present moment?"

"It would look like . . . well, it would look like a poor attachment style or an unintegrated shadow. Maybe it would look like a whole bunch of negative communication habits."

"I can see you've been doing a lot of reading again!"

"I know, I know. It's just that I guess I'm afraid that since I'm dating someone now, and it's looking pretty serious . . . I don't want to mess that up with all my drama and baggage."

"Do you have drama and baggage?"

"Doesn't everyone?"

Dr. Amanda lifted her eyebrows quizzically, and Leah contemplated her own question.

"You already know I'm a CBT therapist, Leah, and that means that although I can recognize the impact of the past, what I'm really interested in is the present—because that's the one and only place where any of us has any power to do what counts. What counts is taking action. I always have this little joke I tell my clients, where I say I won't be happy until my parents treated me better as a kid. It's a joke, but I think it really drives home the point. Even if there is a whole bunch of nasty trauma—baggage and drama, as you say—what does it help to talk about what is gone and cannot be changed?"

"But surely you're not saying that the past doesn't matter, that we should all just move on since we can't do anything about it? Doesn't the past help you understand the present?"

"Of course it does. But let me tell you a story. Imagine if you were walking across the road one day, and a car ran you over. There you were, lying in the street with broken bones and bleeding everywhere. Someone calls an ambulance to come and help you. But when the ambulance arrives, the driver just hops out and comes to talk to you. He asks you all sorts of questions—what kind of car ran you over? Who was driving it? How fast was the car going when it hit you? Was it an accident or did the driver mean it? On and on he quizzes you while you lay there in the road bleeding to death. You tell him impatiently that you need to go to the hospital and be treated. You tell him to just help you already, and he replies, 'But I'm trying to help you! Doesn't the past help you understand the present? If I can just understand why the car drove you over and how, and exactly how your bones got crushed, then you can start healing . . .'"

"Okay, fair enough. I get your point."

There was a comfortable silence for a moment.

work before I was, I do
a normal, happy relati

"When you tell that s
particular role to play

"Yeah. Kind of like . . .]
laughed.

"And when you're acti
screwup, what are the

"Hmm . . . the rule is: ;
But also, you will nev
huh?"

"Leah, is there any e
problem with your nev

Leah thought for a r
head.

"Has this new guy g
believe that he is unha

She shook her head ag

"Are you unhappy with

She shook it a third tin

"So, here we have tl
better get some more
guy gets close to m
secretly a permanent s

"Pretty much."

"Tell me what's bothering you about this new relationship," asked Dr. Amanda, although she had a feeling she knew what the answer would be.

"I'm just . . . I guess I'm just really happy and I don't want to mess it up."

"How would you mess it up?"

"By being . . . you know, by being me. I've never really been in a proper relationship like this before, and I'm scared that . . ."

"Yes?"

"Well, I'm scared that I'll do something wrong."

"Like what?"

"I don't know . . . like he'll get to know me better and just realize that . . . that I'm . . ."

"Can you complete that thought for me? If he gets to know me better, then he'll realize that . . ."

Leah let out a deep sigh. "Then he'll realize that there's something wrong with me." To both her and Dr. Amanda's surprise, Leah then burst out laughing, saying, "Oh God, I'm still carrying that old thing around with me, aren't I?"

Again, the comfortable silence.

"When I think that thought, I feel terrified. I feel like I have to avoid him getting to know me,

make sure that he[...]
reject me. I think [...]
trauma stuff to yo[...]
just figure it all ou[...]
can carry on and [...]
But even as I say t[...]
it is..."

"I'm really impr[...]
here, Leah. You [...]
thought, and all by[...]
were having it, a[...]
pause and exami[...]
such enormous p[...]

"Well, I have you[...]
long time to u[...]
remember once-[...]
China that first ti[...]
once: Having an [...]
going on in the w[...]
an emotional rea[...]
on in your own n[...]
the plane doing j[...]
to something tha[...]
own head. When [...]
I was playing mei[...]

"That's such a gre[...]

"You know, up u[...]
think I had just be[...]
story—all about [...]
was damaged an[...]

"Leah, do you think the issue here is that you have unresolved childhood trauma?"

She shifted in her chair, uncomfortable. "But all the things that happened to me in childhood ... they did actually happen, Dr. Amanda."

"I'm sure they did. But what does it mean that they happened? We get to decide how we talk about them. The story we tell about it."

The woman chatted for a few minutes more, but Leah was now deep in thought and distracted. Was there a way to acknowledge and legitimize everything she'd been through as a child but without it meaning that she was a "permanent screwup"? As the session drew to a close, Dr. Amanda and Leah bid one another adieu for the second time. This time was different, though, but Leah couldn't exactly put her finger on why. All she knew was that she suddenly didn't want to go to therapy ever again. This wasn't an angry or resentful feeling, though. She felt a deep pang of appreciation and gratitude for Dr. Amanda—but she also didn't want to see her again.

Leah left the therapy room that day feeling a little like a small child who impatiently told their parent, "No, don't help me! I can do it myself!" Leah wanted to write her own narrative now. Dr. Amanda had taught her so many things, but now Leah had her own "inner therapist," and this voice had its own unique wisdom, its own values, its own intuition, and its own

Be willing to tolerate uncertainty and the fact that sometimes, you just don't know!

Thought Challenging and Restructuring

When you've identified a recurrent negative thought, become curious about ways you can adjust it so that it is less "personal, pervasive, and permanent." Look for ways the thought might be a distortion—for example, it may be an exaggeration or a minimization, it may be an instance of black-and-white, all-or-nothing thinking, it may be overly harsh and critical, it may be employing bias and filtering, emotional reasoning, or a combination of all of these.

Try to rewrite this thought to make it kinder, more rational, more useful, or more accurate. Keep an eye open for absolute words like *always*, *everything*, *nobody*, and strong language like hate or failure. Watch out for unrealistic expectations and unreasonable demands on yourself hiding behind words like *should* or *must*. There tends to be a much more moderate way to frame these painful thoughts and perceptions.

ABC Analysis

Pay attention to how your automatic thoughts, your feelings, and your actions/behaviors are connected, all mutually influencing one another. If you identify a thought, in particular, ask how it makes you feel, and the type of behavior it tends to encourage in you. Similarly, ask how your feelings and behaviors are in turn creating and sustaining certain thought patterns, catching you in a vicious cycle of reinforcement.

Task Separation

There is a straightforward way to understand the concept of task separation, and it's sometimes referred to as discerning whose "business" is whose. For example, negative automatic thoughts could center around what someone else might be or should be thinking, when in reality it is simply not our responsibility what that person thinks or feels. Those who are prone to people-pleasing or chasing external validation may take on too much responsibility and assume blame for things that really have nothing to do with them.

If others dislike you, whose "fault" is that? Nobody's. It's not your job to get to work convincing them that they're wrong, or making up for it as though their negative feeling says something directly about you. Other people's opinions of us are their business. Our opinions of them are our own business. Becoming very clear about who owns what is a great source of strength for people overly dependent on external validation. It helps us set better boundaries, abstain from blame or unnecessary martyr behavior, and communicate clearly and effectively. You can start to separate tasks by asking yourself, whose goal/task/responsibility/feeling is this? It is only your job to focus on what is *yours*.

Labeling Emotions

Becoming emotionally literate is about increasing awareness and understanding ourselves better—so we can act with full consciousness and free will. When you're feeling overcome with negative emotions, deliberately take the time to pause and look within to try to understand what is happening with you—without judgment, interpretation, or the desire to fix or flee.

A good way to start with this is just to locate sensations in your body. Then, try to pinpoint your feeling along the "emotional primary colors"—fear, happiness, sadness, disgust, surprise, or anger. Once you've identified broadly what you feel, you can use a list of feeling-words (or the "emotion wheel") to further refine exactly what you're experiencing. Take care to discern between your primary emotion (your reaction to a situation) and your secondary emotion (your reaction to your reaction).

Cognitive Defusion

Thoughts can feel overwhelming when we fuse with them, i.e., when we wholly identify with them to the degree that we forget that they are not permanent and do not completely define us in every way. When Leah wrote her thoughts and feelings down on a piece of paper and then physically and literally set them aside on a chair, she was defusing from these thoughts and feelings and experiencing how much easier it was to think, and how much more of the world she could take in when those thoughts and feelings were not so front and center. One easy way to defuse is simply to change a statement like "I'm sad" to "I'm feeling sad right now." This immediately creates a tiny amount of psychological distance.

Behavioral Experiments

Dr. Amanda asked Leah to actually test out her assumptions and theories about herself. Leah made a prediction, ran an experiment, and noticed that the outcome did not match her prediction—this experience is a great way to start challenging automatic assumptions. If you tend to make your own predictions in this way, challenge yourself to literally test them out and see if they hold any water. Maintain an open, curious state of mind and be willing to be surprised. Sometimes, the ability to say "I don't know" is the sanest, most rational position!

Shame-Attacking Exercises

These are the so-called "banana experiments" according to Leah. We do these slightly embarrassing things not because we want to humiliate ourselves, but to prove that our catastrophic worst-case-scenario fears are very seldom accurate. In fact, we can make a fool of ourselves and survive perfectly well—even finding the experience exhilarating. Start small and dare yourself to do little things in your world that your brain has convinced you will result in total annihilation. Give yourself the *lived experience* of this assumption simply not being true.

Mindfulness

Rather than a separate technique, mindfulness and awareness are threaded through every exercise, every question, every moment we pause to check in with ourselves. Give yourself space and be patient. Don't rush. Spend time just noticing where you are, how you feel, and what is cluttering up your head. Contemplate things you don't ordinarily register. There is a space, right here in every moment, where you can be still and feel that full, rich potential to act . . . or to continue being still. Just feel that moment, here and there. Notice how, no matter what happens, you can always return to that moment, and it's always there, waiting for you, exactly as it was when you left it . . .

Grounding

A related technique is to consciously ground in the five senses—sight, sound, touch, taste, and hearing—in order to bring you more fully into the real present and away from anxious rumination that only carries you all over the past, the future, and unreal hypotheticals. Tether your awareness to your sensory experience. You don't have to appreciate them or find them beautiful or relaxing—you just need to fully hand over your consciousness to them and allow them to absorb you for a moment. Nothing will pull you out of an anxiety spiral faster than pausing and checking in with your world via your senses.

Breathing Exercises

Dr. Amanda taught Leah to breathe in, hold it, and breathe out again in a fixed, counted rhythm. It's not the counting that matters, though; it's the focused awareness and the stillness this brings. You can do the same thing by simply focusing on the gentle in and out of the breath, or just watch the breath doing what it will, but focus on nothing else but that sensation. Tune everything else out and just embody each breath as it comes and then falls away again. A few minutes of mindful breathing like this a handful of times through the day will drastically lower anxiety.

Affirmations

Dr. Amanda never "prescribed" any affirmations for Leah, and you may guess why. If you like the sound of affirmations, choose something that is genuinely meaningful to you, or a conscious reworking of an automatic negative thought you've already identified. Try not to introduce cognitive distortions into the affirmations themselves—this is just extending the problem! So, for example, instead of an affirmation like "Every day and in every way, I'm getting better and better" (completely unrealistic and liable to lead to disappointment and shame), say something like, "I await each new day with gratitude and curiosity, whatever it may bring."

Self-Monitoring

Leah experienced the pain of comparing herself to a social media star. Dr. Amanda redirected this impulse toward something more helpful: increasing awareness of our own progress relative to ourselves and our own values and principles. Dr. Amanda encouraged Leah to think about her goals and what was most important, and forget about comparing herself to others—always a losing strategy. Doing so allows us to derive validation internally and to be compassionate with ourselves. Keep track of how you're doing by regularly checking in, writing a diary, or talking to someone you trust. We can forget to appreciate just how far we've come! Take a moment here and there to appreciate the ground you've covered—this encourages self-appraisal that is kind and realistic rather than critical.

Behavioral Activation

Not shown in the above chapters is a common technique used by therapists to help shift clients out of stagnant patterns of depression and anxiety. For a very brief summary of how to use it yourself, simply become aware for a full week or two of all the activities you spend your time on—including things like sleep, commuting, TV, chores, and so on. Simultaneously note how you feel before, during, and after, as well as your overall mood and energy levels, and the things that most consistently hold your attention.

After a week or two, tally up the data to get an idea of 1) how much of your time is going to each activity and 2) how each activity is impacting you. The patterns you discover may be illuminating. For example, you may discover that even though you claim to value your family more than anything, that you only spend about five percent of your waking hours with them, all the while wasting hours every day online and watching TV—an activity you can see leaves you irritable and depressed. Behavioral activation means seeing these patterns and committing to making changes in line with what we know we value, what keeps us healthy and happy, and what undermines us. In this example, we may commit to deliberately cutting TV and internet time and setting some goals for quality time with the family and noticing what changes this brings about.

Identify what you value and what makes you happy, then make a plan and commit to it. That may mean scheduling time to engage with others, do healthy physical activities, get out of the house and into the community, or engage in hobbies and activities. Reflect on how you feel afterward and adjust accordingly. Similarly, notice how you feel after certain behaviors, such as scrolling mindlessly on social media for hours, lounging on the sofa, binging, drinking, spending the weekend alone, and so on. In the moment, these activities may seem like what you "want," but on further reflection, they are not in the least aligned with your values and goals.

Journaling

Any and all of these exercises can be run in conjunction with journaling, which is a place to keep track of our development, slow down our thoughts so we can work through them, complete worksheets, work through prompts and exercises, makes plans and goals, "dump" our chaotic thoughts, practice worry postponement, and more. The great thing about journaling is that it's a discipline and a practice, and if done for long enough, can help us identify larger, overarching patterns we might not otherwise see in ourselves.

Acceptance

Accepting *what is* can prove to be the most challenging part of therapy, and something that many clients want to escape, avoid, or postpone—sometimes they convince their therapists to help them do it! Acceptance doesn't mean we agree with or condone what we don't like, and it doesn't mean we strongly attach to negative feelings and thoughts, either. Sometimes, acceptance can simply look like being brave enough to face facts, tell the truth, and be frank about what is and isn't in your control.

Identifying Values

When doing cognitive restructuring, people talk about reworking old automatic thoughts into ones that are more rational, useful, or realistic. But how do you know what counts as rational, useful, or realistic? It's never the therapist's job to tell you what you should care about or what your priorities are. But without deeply held convictions about what we think is important in life, we cannot engage in life in a meaningful way. It's important to remember, too, that values can and do change over the course of a lifetime, and that your priorities today won't necessarily always be your priorities.

Worry Postponement

It's human to worry sometimes. But be conscious of what you're doing, be aware of what it costs you, and continually ask yourself if you want to go down that path of rumination or not. Worry postponement brings back awareness and a sense of agency to what can often feel like an out-of-control situation. Constantly remind yourself that *you* are in charge, and *you* choose what to do with your mind at any particular moment. Always be cognizant of just how much worry is helping you or improving your life. The more awareness you bring to your overthinking habit, the more it will become clear to you that it brings you, well, nothing.

Practice the worry postponement that Dr. Amanda suggested for Leah, and you'll soon convince yourself that worry is a waste of time—and you don't even enjoy it, anyway!

Taking Action

The final "exercise" we have on this list is arguably the most important one. It's to act. Not think about acting, or talk about acting, or plan to act—but act. None of us is all-powerful, and the world is a complex place—we will not always get the results we want, and often, making our way through the world is difficult, exhausting, and confusing. But if any of the above exercises are to truly be of any use to us, we must carry them outside the therapy room, outside the pages of the journal, outside the confines of our own skulls, and out there, into the world.

Insight, healing, understanding, compassion, acceptance, and awareness are all extremely valuable and important.

But there is no power greater in the universe than the right action at the right time.

www.ingramcontent.com/pod-product-compliance
Lightning Source LLC
Chambersburg PA
CBHW060605080526
44585CB00013B/686